THE ART OF NAPPING

THE ART OF NAPPING

THE SLEEPING SAMURAI AND
THE DORMANT DRAGON

FRANKLIN SOOHO LEE

NEW DEGREE PRESS

COPYRIGHT © 2017 FRANKLIN LEE
All rights reserved.

THE ART OF NAPPING
The Sleeping Samurai and The Dormant Dragon

ISBN   978-1-64137-008-0 *Paperback*
         978-1-64137-009-7 *Ebook*

I dedicate this book to the many sleepless nights, morning catnaps, coffee, energy drinks, melatonin, sofa beds, and friends and family who have helped me get to the present day alive.

CONTENTS

PART ONE
    INTRODUCTION 13

PART TWO
1. SLEEP REVOLUTION 31
2. SLEEP, BEAUTY, AND MONEY 51
3. THE SLEEPING SAMURAI AND THE DORMANT DRAGON .. 69
4. INNOVATION IN SLEEP, NAPS, AND HEALTH 87
5. THE EMERGING SLEEP AND NAPPING INDUSTRY 109
6. BRAVE SLEEP WORLD 127

PART THREE
    CONCLUSION 141
    ACKNOWLEDGEMENTS 149
    SELECTED BIBLIOGRAPHY 151

*"If your sleeping hours are random,
so will be your day."*

— RAVI TEJA VENKATA PEELA, QUORA
WRITER FROM KARNATAKA, INDIA

PART 1

INTRODUCTION

"This is the last time I'm going to procrastinate for a paper," I convinced myself as I unscrewed the cap off my second Five-Hour Energy of the evening and quickly chased it with a Red Bull.

I thought I was becoming an expert in sleep, but in reality, I was an expert in sleep *avoidance*.

As a junior in college, I was majoring in East Asian Studies and Anthropology. The day following my three-Five-Hour-Energy-and-two-Red-Bull all-nighter, I would emerge like a bear after hibernation, except I could only envy the bear's months of sleep. The light was my enemy, but I felt a bit of pride knowing I had fought back the night and won. I had turned in my paper and was pretty sure the professor would think I had spent the past couple weeks on it.

I had really only started it at 6 p.m. the evening prior.

That particular morning wasn't atypical. But it would actually lead me to a conversation that would reveal my obsession with sleep — and no, not sleep avoidance — as one of the most powerful and misunderstood life forces. My tired self had no idea this particular all-nighter would change my life.

I walked (more like stumbled) into the college dining hall, groggy and tired due to my procrastination on yet another paper. Like many college students, I started the semester telling myself that I would start my research early and divide up the work evenly throughout the upcoming weeks, but I would always find myself staring at the computer a couple nights before due dates, red-eyed with a cup of coffee right beside me.

That particular day, I sat next to a friend who was talking to another student. I recognized her face because I had seen her throughout campus, but I had never talked to her before. She explained that she was applying for a school grant to bring nap pods from Japan to our university's campus. At the time, I was saving up so that I could go to Japan with my mother right after graduating. It had been a long-term dream of hers to visit. Additionally, my East Asian Studies classwork had prepped me with various cocktail party-worthy cultural and historical facts.

She explained that Japan was one of the most sleep-deprived countries in the world and that these "nap pods" were becoming popular. Recognizing that many Harvard students are sleep-deprived, she said that she hoped to bring these nap pods to Cambridge so that students could sleep in more convenient locations throughout campus. That night, I went back to my room and started my research on these fascinating machines. Soon enough, I archived a couple of articles that listed nap pods as one of Japan's odd but promising inventions.

But I was too busy to actually read them.

Instead, I read another article about a man named Jim Jasper who was suing a hospital for overworking his wife to death. According to the report, his wife, Beth Jasper, may have fallen asleep while driving after a 12-hour shift. The young nurse could no longer wake up each morning to tell her husband and two children that she loved them.

Years later, I still hadn't read the napping articles I'd archived, and my sleep habits had remained the same: seeing sleep as an enemy to be conquered.

I'd come to Washington, D.C., to get my master's in Asian Studies from Georgetown. Even then, as someone who had "grown up" and graduated college, I hadn't outgrown all-nighters.

One morning, I boarded my morning bus, and I was groggy having not had my coffee yet. About half the time, I fell asleep on the bus, and I'd even missed my stop more than once. I saw the person who occupied the seat before me had left a copy of *The Washington Post* there.

"Maybe reading the paper could become my new routine," I thought. "I'll read it and hopefully won't sleep through the ride or miss my stop."

I settled in and smiled a bit, thinking how the others on the bus might look at me a bit like a grown up — I was reading the paper, after all.

That's when I saw it:

> "Would you pay for a 20-minute nap? This studio is charging $15 for one."

It was almost as if the article had been written especially for me.

And suddenly, I was jolted back to that conversation a few years back in a Harvard dining hall about nap pods.

recharj®, the company featured in the article, was offering power-napping sessions in their meditation centers. I looked at the article more closely to see if they mentioned utilizing nap pods in their space.

They weren't.

"Why?" I wondered.

I tore the page out of the paper as I leapt out of the bus. "Maybe this really is a sign," I thought.

When I'd first begun my master's studies, I had sought to improve my time management so that I could have a better relationship with sleep and my overall health. I recognized that during college, I was constantly sleep-deprived, and my friends even came to know me for my addiction to coffee and Red Bull. When I started grad school, I thought it would be different. Yet the competitive pressure once again forced me into an incredibly busy schedule. With five classes and an internship, my first year passed in a blur. Luckily, after a year of insanity, I was able to reduce my course load to three classes and another internship during the second year.

The reason the article had given me pause was because I was at a breaking point. My need to read a newspaper in order to avoid missing my stop on my morning bus ride was bordering on ridiculous.

The fact that I had less work during this period actually caused me to break down. During my first year, I had been so busy that I didn't even have the time to think about how little I was sleeping. I'd even considered medicating myself — maybe with sleep aids, maybe with Adderall or whatever else I could think of to stop the struggle. Then, with a little more time on my hands during my second year, I suddenly started to realize that I was tired. Not just tired, but exhausted. Not just exhausted, but desperate ... desperate because I was in a potentially dangerous situation. I struggled to finish that semester and realized that I was truly "burnt out."

I was honestly worried.

I'd started to get headaches when I hadn't had caffeine within a four-hour period.

My heart would pound as I lay down at night.

I'd been called out by a professor when I fell asleep in class, not to mention I'd fallen asleep on the bus regularly and missed my stop multiple times.

I was worried something bad could happen to me.

That winter break, I booked a plane ticket back to Los Angeles to try to get some rest in my home, Koreatown. I wasn't sure what I wanted to do after I graduated from my program the next semester. I had applied to some programs hoping to get a job in government, but with Trump's election and the hiring freeze, the job prospects in that area didn't seem too promising.

Still tired and stressed and feeling the physical effects of chronically poor sleep habits, I realized that I needed help. I reflected on a popular Korean proverb, *saeongjima*, which means, "Look at your troubles as a chance for success." This made me think of another Korean proverb, "Even if the sky falls, there is always a hole to rise up in it."

Rise.

"Fitting," I thought.

I suddenly recognized a source of inspiration calling my name.

**

If my tired, exhausted, desperate, and dangerous state was what it would take for me to recognize my problem, it was the moments of calm at home that made me realize the solution might be much closer than I'd imagined.

Japan and China.

Yes, they had been the focus of my studies for the past half decade, but it turned out they were also at the center of a sleep revolution.

For Japan, there was the "rising sun" depicted in their national flag.

Meanwhile, China's rapid economic growth has often been associated with the image of a dormant dragon waking up from its long slumber.

With the economic rise of both East Asian countries, scholars and popular culture have linked various analogies and images to symbolize their growth.

What I noticed at the time was a personal struggle that seemed universal among college students: sleep deprivation. The two images in the flags seemed to be sending me a message of a need for "awakening." In Japan, the rising sun suggests that the country is "waking up" to meet the new world. In the case of China's dormant dragon, the clear image is the awakening of a large serpent, ready to pounce on the new era. These two images were the source of my inspiration: the transition from dark to light, from slumber to wakefulness.

I made a personal promise to myself:

1. I was going to fix myself and my unhealthy obsession with a lifestyle that led me to sleep deprivation.
2. I was going to share my sleep strategies with the millions of college students and young professionals like me who are struggling with the same cultural obsession that makes rest impossible.

I was going to find a solution to my own problems, and I was committed to share that solution with everyone.

And that story is the backbone of this book: how I was letting sleep — more specifically the lack of it — slowly kill me and what I was going to do to change my own relationship with sleep.

Remember earlier how I shared the huge sleep-related issues affecting companies and their workers?

I poured over everything I could find about sleep, napping, sleep research, physiology, and sleep deprivation. It quickly became my obsession. And the craziest part is that the key to increased worker productivity, retention, and overall health may be right in front of us: naps.

> Naps are the solution to billions in worker health premiums and billions in lost worker productivity.

What I found in my research was incredible. By offering

options to nap in the workplace, businesses could help increase the health, happiness, and success of their workers, all while saving money. I am here to share the research with you and tell you the secrets to hacking your sleep.

My Asian Studies experience has actually positioned me perfectly to figure out how the United States might import the best of the world's knowledge about sleep. While I'd started my break at home feeling lost and depressed, I'd emerged a month later with a new mission and passion: fixing sleep for American youth like me.

My sleep research was actually pretty compelling. My college conversation and the article I'd seen in *The Washington Post* had been foreshadowing for my newfound purpose.

If I wanted to start a business to help solve the sleep crisis, all roads pointed to napping — nap pods, more specifically. And I read and researched constantly. Ironically enough, I'd started to lose sleep thinking about sleep. Napping became an obsession, a topic that I could talk about for hours on end.

As it turns out, my timing couldn't have been better. In 2016, Arianna Huffington, cofounder and editor-in-chief of the Huffington Post, published a bestselling book called *The Sleep Revolution: Transforming Your Life One Night at a Time*. What was more surprising to me was that in the first chapter of her book, Huffington shared the term for "death from overwork" in East Asian societies, a term that does not exist in the English language. Referencing the Japanese (*karoshi*), Chinese (*gulaosi*), and Korean (*gwarosa*) terms for this concept, she introduced her story by pointing to the issue of sleep deprivation in Asia.

How does this all connect, and what do I, a first generation Korean immigrant, have to offer to you?

In my years at Harvard, I did everything but nap. I used energy drinks and melatonin to control my sleep schedule. I thought of every possible way to work more hours. Ironically, I learned that the ultimate strategy to work more was to work less. Instead of increasing the hours I worked, I should have worked fewer hours and reserved that time to nap.

Napping was the ultimate hack to raising my grades, networking effectively with friends, and living a happier life.

Naps: These are the changes that every employer must bring to their employees. Yes, you heard that right. Employers need to encourage their employees to nap at work.

Why? Well, just take a look the following statistics:

- Every year, the U.S. loses $411 billion in GDP due to sleep deprivation in workers.
- Lack of sleep results in a loss of 1.2 million working days for U.S. companies in a single year.
- Sleep loss increases health costs by increasing one's chances of heart attack, kidney disease, diabetes, and stroke.

This book offers employers and employees a shared plan to first understand the science of sleep and then learn how to create more effective workers and work through sleep management.

Napping changed my life by helping me improve not only my academic performance but also my emotional intelligence, health, and general well-being.

This will show you that naps are the key to ameliorating the corporate productivity crisis and big parts of the U.S. health crisis, as well as providing an economic boon for companies.

My training as an anthropologist gave me the perfect framework to bring insights from one culture to another. An anthropologist's task is to "make the strange familiar, and the familiar strange." Growing up as a Korean American in Los Angeles with parents who could not speak English, part of my lifelong journey has been bridging the various cultural differences that I was exposed to.

For instance, throughout my childhood, my aunt who is also an immigrant from South Korea would talk about how students would prop their eyelids open with toothpicks to keep themselves awake. My mother would remind me that students in South Korea would check if their neighbors' lights were turned off as a way of gauging how many hours the other students were studying each night. In various ways, these stories have shaped how I view the world around me, perhaps in very different ways than students who have no connection to the Asian continent.

Different stories and experiences can drastically shape our understanding of the world. At the same time, they can heavily impact our daily decisions and approaches to life. I believe that one of America's greatest strengths is that it facilitates cultural exchanges between people from all around the world. Culture isn't owned by a society or an ethnic group. It is shared, modified, and developed over time. This book will delve into a culture that hasn't been highly recognized for much of our history despite its importance to our daily lives: sleep.

To this day, many Americans might find the concept of a nap pod odd. However, to me, it is the future. Nap pods are part of a revolutionary culture that is sweeping our society. Years back, I remember seeing selfie sticks for the first time in Jeju Island while doing field research for my undergraduate thesis. While staying with my other roommates at a hostel, I still remember the one man with the selfie stick animatedly explaining the item's purpose to all of the curious roommates. Years later, I find selfie sticks everywhere. They're not limited to use by South Koreans and have reached European and American travelers as well.

Similarly, I see the sleep or napping industry as a growing trend — no, a cultural revolution — heading into American society. Terry Cralle, certified clinical sleep educator, published a book in 2016 titled *Sleeping Your Way to the Top: How to Get the Sleep You Need to Succeed*. Speaking with Cralle, I learned that she had struggled to publish her book about five years back. However, by the time she was looking for a publisher a couple years ago, the reaction to a book about the need for sleep had completely changed: Publishers were instead competing for her book. Finally, the publishers had realized that the sleep revolution was here to stay.

Ultimately, my point is that lack of sleep is becoming a global issue. As the world is becoming more urban and its citizens more competitive, sleep deprivation is now a health epidemic bound to become more serious in the upcoming years. Humans have developed various technologies and cures to address major societal problems through the ages. It is my firm belief that our major societal problem today is sleep deprivation, which is the reason why I have pursued this research. With the content of this book, I hope to become a part of a larger community addressing one of the largest issues of our time. Recent innovations in sleep and naps like nap pods will revolutionize the world in the same way that cars and lightbulbs have transformed the world as we know it.

In many ways, napping saved my life. Sure, I didn't have a "near death" experience like Beth. Thankfully, it didn't get to that level of severity for me, but I know I was on that path.

I can now confidently say that through my research on and experiences with sleep, I am dedicated to improving worker productivity and solving the health crisis jointly affecting the American company and worker.

This story shares my own journey toward a life of sleep health and a path toward a sustainable culture that celebrates sleep, offering every American the tools to embark on the same journey.

PART 2

CHAPTER 1

SLEEP REVOLUTION

The samurai and the dragon were enjoying a peaceful afternoon together when they somehow entered into a quarrel.

The dragon boasted of his strength and his flames' ability to wipe out the samurai in an instant.

Meanwhile, the samurai claimed that the dragon was too slow and dim-witted to win a fight.

The samurai said, "I have never missed my daily trainings, sleeping less than four hours a night to ensure that I am always at top form."

The dragon quickly retorted, "Instead of sleeping, I torch my cave each night so that I can admire my shadow bursting out volcanic flames and my immense wings that can root out any tree with one gust."

Back and forth, they boasted of their incredible battles, their agility and strength, and their superiority over the other until they exclaimed, "I challenge you to a match!"

Content with the proposal, they smirked at each other.

"Tomorrow evening, right here!" the dragon roared.

"I'll be here!" shouted the samurai.

In an instant, the samurai turned his back while the dragon slithered away in the other direction.

The samurai returned to his cottage realizing that he had spent too much adrenaline arguing with the dragon. He was tired.

"I must finish my training for tomorrow's match," he told himself. He looked at the ascetic but pristine bed inside his room. "But perhaps a 10-minute nap wouldn't hurt." Without changing his clothes, he lay down and closed his eyes. In an instant, he started snoring.

Meanwhile, the dragon had just returned to the dark cave where he lit up the torches around him. He admired the ferocious and *frightening shadows reflecting his large wings and tail. After a couple of minutes admiring his various forms, he curled into a ball to test how small he could make himself. This time, the shadow remained without changing form until the torches ran out of fire.*

**

While this may not come as a surprise, the inventor of the lightbulb Thomas Edison regularly demonized sleep. In fact, throughout his lifetime, he frequently argued that humans could "learn to live without it." In an 1889 interview with *Scientific American*, Edison claimed that he not only slept four hours a day but also enforced that same rule for his employees. In the book *The Diary and Sundry Observations of Thomas A. Edison*, Dagobert D. Runes quotes Edison as having said, "I never found need of more than four or five hours' sleep in the twenty-four. I never dream. It's real sleep."

To give him some credit, various sources at the time confirmed that he slept only three to four hours every night. Seeing as he slept so little and was still very successful, many people likely found him qualified to preach that "sleep" was a waste of time, "a heritage from our cave days."

To no surprise, the discussion of our world's stigma against sleep starts from the person who arguably disrupted our internal clocks.

Perhaps contrary to one's intuition, however, there were other forms of artificial lights before Edison. In 1736, London used 5,000 gas lights in the streets to keep shops open past 10 p.m. Even throughout the Civil War, New York City had so many gas lamps that people commonly walked out at night in the same way that you might see people out and about in the city during the late evening today.

There is no doubt, however, that the invention of the lightbulb revolutionized the world by making artificial light accessible to the common household at an affordable price. For people today, it is probably difficult to imagine a world without artificial light in the night — hopefully a bit more difficult to imagine than a life without iPhones.

Clearly, Edison was ahead of his time. He may have very well imagined a world with artificial light because of his night-owl habits. In some interviews of his early childhood friends, one friend recalled Edison staying up every night to read about mechanics, chemistry, and electricity.

Throughout his life, Edison believed that the invention of the lightbulb would eliminate the need for sleep, saying that in the same way people tend to overeat, they oversleep because they like it. Arguing that the extra sleep is unhealthy and inefficient, he said that people who slept for eight to ten hours a day weren't experiencing "real sleep" like him but were merely undergoing light dozing.

What he forgot to mention, however, was his little secret: power napping. In various unusual locations throughout his property ranging from labs to libraries, Edison had set up numerous cots for napping. Perhaps photographers found humor in capturing his hypocrisies, as there are many photographs just a Google search away of Edison napping outdoors, on his cot, and on chairs and stools.

In many records, he was known to take one or two brief naps most days, and people found that he was reinvigorated from his short slumbers rather than groggy.

The reason why I start my narrative with Edison is because as the inventor of the lightbulb, he was a man who prioritized productivity, an obsession that continues in our modern world. While his sleep habits might have stemmed from his DNA rather than his willpower, his experiences with sleep had a profound impact on his life mission and the rest of the world. While I'm not expecting to have as profound an impact as Edison, I present two main goals in my book: to help sleep-deprived workers strategize their lives so that they can sleep more and become more productive and — more importantly — to break the social stigma against sleep.

COMMON MISCONCEPTIONS ABOUT SLEEP

The average person sleeps for a third of the day. That means that if we consider the average lifespan of about 80 years in the U.S., we spend around 27 years of it sleeping (Oh, the horror!).

Of course, this wasn't the case for Edison. When he was 53 years old, he told his interviewer Orison Swett Marden that he no longer worked hard, as he was "only" working 14-15 hours a day compared to 20 hours during his early years. That meant that during his prime he would only sleep about four hours every night, or one-sixth of a day. Again, with the average lifespan of a U.S. resident in mind, that would translate to about 13 years (which is still a lot, I suppose, but it's a bit more reassuring).

Like Edison, I remember staying up much of the night as a child. With artificial light, I guess it was a lot easier. I remember staring at the ceiling listening to my dad's snores while counting sheep. Although I was only four years old at the time, I still remember the many nights I spent wide awake praying that I'd fall asleep at any second. At the time, my parents, my sister, and I all shared the same room with two king beds connected together. After an hour or so, I would kick all the blankets away because of the uncomfortable warmth and cling to the cool, plastered wall in order to let off some of my body heat. A couple of hours later, I would quietly hop out of bed and walk over to the window, where I'd see the clock tower outside signaling that it was past midnight.

I also remember that I would sleep often throughout the day. It was almost as if I could sleep anywhere, any time as long as the sun was up. I would sleep inside the car, on the floor, during my sister's piano recital. Ironically, the only place that I seemed to be having trouble falling asleep was in our family bed.

I now thank my mother for the horrible sleeping genes, although I didn't always feel this level of gratitude. When I was younger, I did not realize how much trouble my mother had going to sleep. When my sister and I were kids, she had simply been too exhausted to lose any opportunity to sleep. However, once we started attending school and she had a bit more freedom with her schedule, she returned to her sleep cycle that she had before we were born. Unlike my dad and sister who would fall asleep almost immediately once they hit the bed, my mother and I had trouble falling asleep at night. During the same quiet, dark hours I was familiar with, my mother would quietly go to the living room and turn on the lamp to read the newspaper. On the other hand, when my father turned on the television, she would immediately fall into an uncontrollable slumber.

What accounted for these differences? Genetics? It all felt so unfair. That was until I started going to school.

As I entered first grade, I realized that I was a natural early riser. Although I still couldn't get myself to sleep at night, I was adept at waking up early. With my newly discovered skill, I quickly became obsessive. Every morning, I sought to be the first student in line as I waited for the teacher to walk us to our classroom. I would always aim to get out to the car by 7:15 a.m. so that I could arrive at school by 7:25 a.m. — about 35 minutes before the school bell. Although I would spend each morning shivering outside alone, I felt a sense of pride thinking that I was the best at something, even if it was small and irrelevant. On the occasional days that I accidentally woke up late, I would wail, blaming my parents for not waking me up on time.

On the other hand, my sister would always struggle to wake up on time every morning. Today, I know that her case is more typical. In fact, it's probably healthier. Since she was five years older than me, there were a number of years where she attended school while I was at home. She would often wake up groggy and tired, refusing to get out of bed by first telling our parents that she was awake before falling asleep again.

At the time, I thought the situation was funny because my sister was an incredibly high-achieving student who was loved by all her teachers and peers. Everyone assumed that she was the "model" child, the precocious pianist, and the perfect Korean-English bilingual speaker. In fact, she was my role model. In comparison, I felt "below average." This might have been the reason that I was so obsessive about being the first to wake up and get to school before my friends did.

It seems that, in hindsight, what my sister practiced was in fact the path toward academic success. Contrary to popular belief, sleep research is showing more and more that children who wake up later perform better at school. There is no better person to learn this from than the accomplished Sean Bruich, vice president of global consumer knowledge at Nike. At the young age of 32, Sean has already worked as a marketing manager at Google before directing research for Facebook as well.

Long before his success, Sean was also a precocious elementary school student who recognized the importance of sleep. With his mother, Harvard-educated sleep expert Dr. Cheryl Spinweber, aiding his research, Sean won a blue ribbon in his county science fair's social science division by collecting data related to how school start times correlate to student performance. His study showed that schools with later start times not only had fewer absences and suspensions but also had fewer kids repeating grades. Sean's science fair project seemed to suggest a revolutionary solution to an important problem in America's education system: more sleep! His study calculated that if all San Diego schools started at or after 8:50, the district would reduce annual absences by 170,000 including the older teens in school. At the time, Sean himself had an average of 9.5 hours of sleep each night. After his middle school science fair, Sean excelled at University City High School and graduated from Stanford University where he counted Dr. William Dement, a world authority on sleep, as one of his professors.

We often hear the phrase "The early bird catches the worm." In fact, our society has ingrained the concept so deeply into our lives that we don't even realize how subtly it is affecting us. Before hearing Sean's story, I did not even consider that it was possible for school to start at a later time. Surely there was a reason why school started early, and there was no way we could change something as fundamental as school hours. On second thought, however, I realized that the concept of school hours was in fact conceptualized before it was implemented. In other words, it simply started early because that's how it was. I think professional boxer George Foreman may have been spot-on with this quote: "I think sleep was my problem in school. If school had started at 4 in the afternoon, I'd be a college graduate today."

MY FIGHT AGAINST OUR SLEEPLESS SOCIETY

When I started middle school, I resolved to change my sleeping habits. This wasn't for the sake of school. At the time, my logic was that sleeping more would help me grow taller.

Shorter than my peers, I thought that increasing the amount of time I spent sleeping would help me grow taller. Just in case you're curious, I'm still quite short at 5'4" despite all the extra sleep I got.

Unfortunately, my plan came with various obstacles. My parents would turn the television on at around 7-8 p.m. each night, and the best program would start around 10 p.m. after the 9 o'clock Korean news. At times, I would stand by the door listening in on the noise of the television. Many other times, my mother would welcome herself into my room without knocking as I was just falling into a relaxing lull, telling me that I had to see what was onscreen. With a room of my own, I set a schedule where I would go to bed by 9 p.m. regardless of whether I was sleepy or not.

During high school, my battles changed. Suddenly, I was fighting to stay awake later into the night. Every night, I sighed at the amount of work I had to get done for the next day. Around the time my parents would go to bed, they would come to my room to check in with me and try and convince me to go to bed.

One day, a gifted friend of mine who graduated a year early came back from college to visit me. She said, "College life is the following, you can only choose two of the three: social life, grades, and sleep."

Genuinely curious, I asked, "What would you choose?"

After some thinking, she said, "I think I would sacrifice sleep."

I nodded my head in complete agreement.

As a senior in high school, I had been secretly stealing the coffee packets from the kitchen counter to keep myself awake at night. While my caffeine-addicted mother was adamant that she would protect my sister and me from this "dangerous" substance, I had already fallen under the pressure of studying for the SATs and AP classes. At high school, I had many nights where I felt completely defeated because I had so much work to do. I often found myself at loss as to how I would ever finish all of my assignments.

At Harvard, I took my caffeine addiction to new levels. With the unlimited coffee in the dining halls, I also added tea, coke, Red Bull, and five-hour energy drinks to my intake. While attending office hours one day, I chatted with a Ph.D. student about my addiction and she joked, "I had a check-up at the hospital and the doctor said, 'Good news is that I still see some blood left in your veins.'"

Meanwhile, these jokes were building up to very serious issues. First, with weekly dictations for my Chinese class, I realized that sleep was the best way to consolidate my vocabulary and study a language that requires so much rote memorization. Additionally, with my busy schedule, my grades in Chemistry and Linear Algebra were stupefyingly low. I ended up with an nonsensical GPA my first year at college.

To this day, sleep-related humor is bittersweet for me. From "You can sleep once you're in your coffin" to "Laugh and the world laughs with you, snore and you sleep alone," college seemed to place sleep at the very bottom of our hierarchy of needs. Today, I realize that sacrificing sleep to be successful is a dangerous concept. In fact, it is the path to an unhealthy and sickly society.

Meanwhile, the idea of returning back to a life before "artificial light" is also problematic. In the 1800s in Europe and America, people had no reason to think that they needed a full eight hours of uninterrupted sleep to be productive.

In that sense, our standard or ideal sleep schedule is a relatively new innovation. Roger Eskirch's essay "Sleep We Have Lost: Pre-Industrial Slumber in the British Isles" explained that standard nighttime sleep in most of Europe and North America across a wide range of nationalities and social classes was to have two shifts of "segmented sleep" where one would have "dead sleep" before bridging it to "morning sleep." In his essay, Ekirsch argued that people should revert back to two-shift sleep because it was the more "natural" form of sleep. His reasoning was that with the intervention of artificial lighting, the time between the two shifts of sleep became a loss of valuable time for sleep.

His article became controversial but popular at the time, as his argument felt coherent and logical. In 1911, one American newspaper advice column counseled readers to take two shifts in their sleep, reminding them of their previous sleep pattern.

Since the publication of his article, a couple more articles have sprung up taking positions against his statements. Pointing to different societies like those of Tanzania, Namibia, and Bolivia that didn't show signs of segmented sleep before the introduction of artificial light, scientists argued that one should not be so rash as to categorize all people into one sleeping pattern, especially with the focus of only one or two regions.

Humans have a tendency to romanticize our history. From the "Paleo Diet" that suggests we revert back to our ancestral diet before agriculture to bringing manufacturing jobs back to the U.S. — as our current president Donald Trump often suggests — people often understand the past in the context of the present. I believe that there are certain benefits of the Paleo Diet. I also realize that the unemployment rate in the U.S. has been rising while we are importing more products and services from abroad. However, the logic deduced from facts is often flawed and fundamentally problematic in the same way that it is wrong to assume the cavemen followed a strict Paleo Diet, or that the manufacturing jobs worldwide are in fact jobs that Americans had decades ago. As time passes, the world changes. As the context for the issues we face changes, so must our solutions; returning to the past is not the best solution. The best we can do is understand the past as a reference while considering the situation at the time.

Today, the issue of sleep deprivation is not one that calls for humans to revert back to prehistoric times. There is no guarantee that the sleep cycles of our ancestors were ideal. While historical records and ongoing sleep research brings us a lot of information to process so that we can better understand sleep, the goal of this book is not to convince readers that we must revert to the past. Rather, it is to look forward. What is the future of sleep? Why is it important? What did Edison get wrong? More importantly — if we are aspiring to become the modern, always-productive individuals epitomized in the present world — what did he get right?

INTRODUCTION TO SLEEP RESEARCH

Terry Cralle, author of *Sleeping Your Way to the Top*, immediately seemed active and energetic in her demeanor when I met her. Her voice was pleasant and enthusiastic. I was thinking to myself that she seemed very well-rested. On the other hand, I was nervous. Although I was elated to be speaking with her, I didn't think that I'd be fortunate enough to interview a published author and expert on sleep a week into my interview process.

Cralle's enthusiasm was luckily contagious, and I soon found myself talking freely with her. She explained that years before when she first submitted her manuscripts to publishers, most of them rejected her telling her that her book would not sell. When she finally secured one, Cralle explained that she had various troubles that caused her to cancel the contract and look for a new publisher. What she said next was surprising. By that time — a couple of years after she had first signed the contract — publishers were suddenly receptive to the content of her book. In fact, they were vying to get her book published.

Cralle's comments brought about an interesting discussion because I realized that I was part of a similar trend. On one occasion, I sat on the toilet seat inside Georgetown's bathrooms to find an interesting poster inside the stall. Every month, the *Stall Seat Journal* would put out a new poster in the washrooms. In this particular poster, there were drawings of cute sheep: a napping sheep, a sheep with glasses with a laptop, and a sheep on a treadmill. With the theme of "Saxa Shuteye," the poster presented some numbers to convince students that they should sleep more, then provided some advice to help them improve the quality of their sleep. According to the poster, a 2014 study revealed that 46% of Georgetown students felt sleepy 3-5 days within the last week. As Cralle had mentioned, our world seemed to very suddenly and desperately need more sleep.

Speaking of the toilet, Cralle also had a bathroom story to share. While explaining the various clients she had while she worked as sleep psychologist, she remembered dealing with one accomplished and seemingly polished female CEO who would use the women's restroom as the only place to recharge. With her hectic schedule, the 10-minute nap next to toilet paper and the smell of ammonia was the only way she could get through her busy day.

During our short chat that afternoon, her message was clear: people were obsessed with productivity, yet they were not obsessed with sleep. With her book and Arianna Huffington's book published in the same year, Cralle thought that the tides were finally turning.

She explained: Consider seeing an individual with a laptop and coffee on their desk. Similarly, imagine seeing someone scribbling notes on their notebook during an important business meeting. What would you think? You would probably assume them to be a hardworking individual. However, what if the person on the laptop had been spending their time looking through Facebook? What if the person furiously scribbling notes was actually doodling?

With that same concept in mind, what would you think if you saw someone sleeping on their desk?

FINAL WORDS ABOUT OBSESSION WITH PRODUCTIVITY

How many times have you heard that a swan — while gracefully moving on a lake — vigorously moves its webbed feet to realize its elegant motion? How many times have you told yourself that you cannot risk the perfect image you have contrived in the work place? And most importantly, how many times have you complained — or rather bragged — about how little sleep you got in the last night or week?

To me, there is no debate regarding whether the world today is obsessed with the idea of productivity. Since I was young, I've been told to start early. Every step along the way, adults would tell me, "You're so much farther ahead than I was when I was a student your age. One day, you're going to be thankful that you worked so hard." As a high school student preparing for the college application process, I remember being told that I should "build up" my summer experiences. At a college-preparatory magnet school, I was provided with various summer opportunities including an internship at a law firm, Dickstein Shapiro, during my sophomore year. With weekly orientations every Friday, we learned how to prepare our resumes so that we could conquer college applications and future job hunts.

Years later after going to college, I came back to visit my high school, where I met with my Calculus BC teacher. During our talk, I shared my experiences from my internship in Santiago, Chile. I don't remember exactly the direction of our conversation, but one of his pieces of advice stuck with me: "It's a skill to look productive." I nodded back, but I had an odd revelation in my head. The concept of actually being productive is different than appearing productive. It is very easy and tempting to imagine that a person is an unproductive slouch — someone who may have gone out to party last Friday night before making their way to their office desk or someone who is terrible with time management, unprofessional, and too lazy to do their hair and makeup for work.

Throughout my early years in school, like the average high school student, I was obsessed with "looking" productive. On some days, I would proudly go to school looking haggard, bragging to my friends that I hadn't slept the night before. At times, I would share my nightly conquest as the Robin Hood of coffee packets with my friends, and at other times, I would carry heavy textbooks between classes instead of leaving them inside the locker, thinking that they made me look smarter.

In hindsight, I am not particularly embarrassed by those memories. In fact, I find them amusing. However, what I do find problematic with these narratives is that I was actually doing it all wrong. I was false advertising.

My mother always recalled her father rushing her to bed, even on nights when she would be cramming for a final the next day. Perhaps due to his influence, she would always encourage me to do the same. While there were the many nights that I would complain that I didn't get enough sleep because my parents were watching television, most nights they were also trying to make sure that I slept well so that I'd be ready for school. Overall, I was probably well-rested compared to some of my peers.

In my mind, there is no doubt that my actions were heavily influenced by societal pressures. To this day, people assume that those who are successful sacrifice sleep to get on top. However, as Cralle suggests in the title of her book, you really have to "sleep your way to the top." The question is "How?" The rest of this book is an attempt to answer that question so that we can utilize sleep to reach our ultimate potential.

Chapter Summary:

- The lightbulb was an incredible invention, although Edison's claim that people can outgrow sleep was false.
- Your sleep can raise your grades. It can also help you land the jobs of your dreams.
- Think a cup of coffee is better than a nap on your desk? Think again.

CHAPTER 2

SLEEP, BEAUTY, AND MONEY

―

The samurai woke up refreshed but anxious about his upcoming match. To make up for his lost time, he immediately started his daily drill. The samurai had perfected every movement and anticipated every move an enemy might draw on him. His sword was razor sharp. His grasp of the hilt was firm but not rigid. He grinned; he was ready, and he knew that he would defeat the dragon.

The dragon slithered out of the cave to find that it was daytime. He spread his wings to make his rounds of the forest so that every animal would be reminded that this was his territory, his kingdom. He had slept a little more than he had intended, but there was nothing to fear. His scales were invincible, and his fire could melt any sword or man. He wasn't worried about winning the match. If anything, he was worried about hurting his little friend.

The entire match was like a piece of art. The samurai bellowed out a war cry while the dragon roared to show the world he was ready. In the same way that the sharp blade of the samurai's sword glistened under the sun, the rays hit the scales of the dragon's large wings, reflecting blinding light.

For hours, they dueled each other. The samurai moved in perfect form, dodging and attacking the dragon left and right, above and below. The dragon was incredibly agile, showing off his mighty wings and swinging his tail. Nature, the duel's only spectator, seemed to admire their beauty as the soft breeze encouraged them to go on, as if they would never stop.

Except they did. Both heaving heavily, the samurai's kimono was wet and dragon's scales were covered with dirt. They stood still without making a move.

Without much energy, they cried out to each other, "Rematch, tomorrow!"

The samurai, exhausted, trudged to his cottage while the dragon seemed unusually lethargic making its way back to the cave. Within a couple of minutes, the samurai was lying in bed while *the dragon coiled up without bothering to scorch his torches and admire his beauty.*

**

While obsession over sleep is still absent in our society, beauty seems to be an obsession worldwide. However, while the U.S. spends $24 billion per year on the beauty industry, this is nothing compared to the industry's prominence in South Korea. While the beauty and personal care market makes up 2.1 percent and 3.9 percent of the GDP in the U.K. and the U.S., respectively, South Korea's beauty market makes up 5.8 percent of the GDP.

With the rise of K-pop as a popular media genre worldwide, South Korea has been receiving a lot of attention for its beauty industry, with cosmetic surgeries being its most controversial asset. With a $5 billion industry, South Korea attracts foreigners worldwide by promising double eyelids, taller noses, daintier chins, and "caterpillar" or *aebeolle* eye bags (yes, they're called caterpillar skin). In 2014, one source estimated that 267,000 foreigners came to South Korea for surgical procedures, spending $468.8 million. Our American media often look at these beauty trends in horror, emphasizing its irrational pain and potential danger. However, as in many cases, this caricature of the matter fails to capture its complexity.

In South Korea as of 2015, 69 percent of 25-34 year olds had a college degree, the highest rate among OECD countries. And yet the number of unemployed South Korean youth has steadily increased from 330,000 in 2013 to 410,000 in the first half of 2015 alone. This means one-third of South Korea's unemployed population has an undergraduate degree. Therefore, even though the 12.5 percent unemployment rate in Seoul, South Korea in 2016 seems relatively small, the unemployment issue in South Korea doesn't reflect that of the rest of the world. In fact, what South Korea is displaying is a phenomenon that the rest of the world is expected to face as the level of education throughout the world rises while the number of jobs available decreases.

This social issue of unemployment fuels the obsession over beauty in South Korea.

Many South Koreans believe that beauty is part of their professional investment. Ji-eun Park, for example, had a nose job and double-eyelid surgery not because she was unhappy with her looks but because she believed that the enhancements were similar to improving her resume. Historically, South Koreans have often referred to *gwansang*, or physiognomy, to foreshadow a person's future. While there was a time when plastic surgery was stigmatized in South Korean society because it was considered to be a sin to damage the face and body given by your ancestors, societal pressure to remain competitive soon altered trends. Looking to plastic surgery as a way to change their future, women and men continue to spend a fortune on beauty procedures.

NAP TO EARN MORE:

At this point, you might ask, "Who cares? I'm not here to read about beauty, I'm here to read about sleep." Well, actually, beauty has a very important correlation to sleep, especially in the context of this book. They're both connected to money!

Various studies worldwide, believe it or not, suggest that people who are better-looking earn more money! At the same time, experiments consistently show that people view well-rested people as more attractive than their tired peers.

What's more, research shows that sleep changes your personality and performance in the workplace.

This brings it down to one simple point: Monetary success is related to beauty, personality, and performance. How do you achieve all three? Sleep more!

Beauty:

Arguably, the story of South Korea's plastic surgery industry comes as a shock to us because we feel that we should not be discriminated against in the workplace due to our looks. By "looks" I mean how attractive you are based on how you are perceived by others. For many, being attractive means that you are more likely to be successful in relationships with friends and romantic partners; it doesn't necessarily indicate that you'd be successful in the workplace, too. I mean, that would be unfair, right?

And yet books like *Beauty Pays: Why Attractive People Are More Successful* by Daniel Hamermesh suggest that people perceived to be attractive are more likely to be employed and have higher pay. Within their lifetime, an attractive person in America might earn $230,000 more than a person with average looks.

The book *Erotic Capital: The Power of Attraction in the Boardroom and the Bedroom* by Catherine Hakim argues that the correlation between attractiveness and one's wage does not discriminate against males or females. In one study by Hamermesh and Biddle, data showed that male lawyers with the highest attractiveness ranking of "5" had an average wage that was 10% higher than that of the male lawyers with a "4" ranking.

The income gap between the "attractive" and the "average" extends beyond the legal profession. Attractive NFL quarterbacks like Tom Brady, Tony Romo, and Tim Tebow earn an average of $300,000 more than "average-looking" quarterbacks with similar statistics.

At this point, it seems that the only thing one can do is look in the mirror and think what an unfair this world is. Before you think to yourself that plastic surgery may be the only option to change your future, what if you learned that you could increase your salary simply by sleeping more?

Some people may already be aware that sleep deprivation results in swollen eyelids, bloodshot eyes, dark circles, and wrinkles near the corner of the mouth. However, studies have found that people's perceived health, attractiveness, and tiredness is much more accurate than we've imagined. In one 2010 study by the British Medical Journal, a group of 65 people consistently rated the attractiveness of 23 people in a way that directly correlated with their sleep-deprived status.

Science helps us understand how sleep deprivation affects us biologically, making such studies easier to comprehend. One study conducted by the University Hospital Case Medical Center in Ohio found that sleep-deprived people lose 30% more water from their skin in the course of 72 hours from exposure to UV light and other skin barrier disruptions than non-sleep-deprived people do. The same study found that poor sleepers were then likely to see twice the amount of aging signs — such as fine lines, uneven pigmentation, reduced elasticity, and slower recovery from sunburn — than average sleepers. Another study by the American Journal of Physiology found that people with obstructive sleep apnea, "a potentially serious sleep disorder in which breathing repeatedly stops and starts during sleep," were more likely to experience weight gain and have trouble losing weight.

There certainly seems to be some truth in the concept of "beauty sleep." However, for those looking for more drastic alterations, one may look to South Korea's cosmetic industry. Today, the most disturbing fact about some of the cosmetic procedures in South Korea is not that many people want to become beautiful through drastic measures but that there is a societal pressure to do so. Both men and women are pressured to undergo expensive and dangerous procedures because they believe they will be treated differently and paid differently. Imagine a world where the government would starve you if you don't become "beautiful."

Imagine a society where being "average" or "unique" is unacceptable. Would you want to live in that society?

In 2005, Scott Westerfeld released a science-fiction novel called *Uglies*, narrating a dystopian world in which everyone is turned "pretty" by extreme cosmetic surgery once they hit age 16. In a world where the government provides for everything, the government also removes the "responsibility for identity" by creating sameness and uniformity among its citizens.

In the story, the characters are taught that their bodies and faces are "temporary" and will eventually be replaced with cosmetic surgery. What is more interesting is that they are taught to connect their features to their personalities, meaning that their personalities change from "ugly" to "pretty" with their physical changes.

Through his narrative, Westerfeld helps his readers think about identity as separate from the beautiful/ugly binary. Somewhat similarly to the message in the phrase "Beauty is in the eye of the beholder," beauty may not be so narrowly defined through a taller nose and larger eyes.

And yet people are drawn to beauty even after realizing that it cannot be so narrowly defined. Beauty, while seemingly superficial, plays an important part in our career success. Recognizing this reality, it is time to change your strategy. Rather than going through drastic measures to change your beauty based on societal expectations, it may be a better idea to add "take a nap" to your beauty regime.

Personality:

Unfortunately, lack of sleep has a range of other health detriments that affect our professional lives apart from our perceived beauty. What if your lack of sleep also affected your personality, making you more irritable and mean? One study conducted by University of North Carolina psychology professor Jane Gaultney found that among the 379 business leaders they followed, those who had the largest gap between weeknight to weekend sleep correlated to lower evaluations of leadership by colleagues and peers. Another study by University of Washington associate professor Christopher Barnes suggested that quality of sleep was as important as quantity of sleep, directly influencing the self-control of leaders. His research suggested that sleep-deprived leaders are more abusive and toxic in their daily interpersonal interactions.

According to similar research published in *Consulting Psychology: Practice and Research*, sleep deprivation may also lower emotional intelligence. Through their study of 104 senior leaders, they found that leaders without enough sleep were less empathetic and warm. Additionally, they were found to lack interpersonal effectiveness compared to leaders who reported little or no sleep loss over a three-month period.

Various research suggests that emotional intelligence is one of the best indicators of our professional success. Throughout my time at Georgetown, I have taken a number of personality tests including Myers-Briggs, StrengthsFinder, and Color Code. However, no matter how great our personalities are inside, studies suggest that they will never make it outside if we do not sleep enough!

If you've ever noticed your mood change when you become sick, then it might be easier to comprehend how sleep affects your daily mood. How happy can you feel when you get the flu? In the peer-edited journal *Sleep*, a recent study suggested that sleep deprivation increases one's risk of developing the common cold since sleep helps regulate our immune systems. People getting less than six hours of sleep each night are four times more likely to catch a cold when exposed to a virus than people who sleep more than seven hours.

If you've ever watched the kid show *Osmosis Jones* which fictionalizes the life of our cells inside our body, then you might be imagining viruses parading around while Osmosis Jones works busily to keep his city inside your body safe. Wrecking your sleep schedule is doing no favors for Osmosis Jones, in case that motivates you stay on top of your sleep.

Performance:

Just to give you a better idea of how drastically your sleep deprivation can affect your mood, one experiment categorized three groups where subjects slept four, six, and eight hours every night. The study found that after two weeks, people with six hours of sleep exhibited behaviors of a person with a blood alcohol level of 0.1%, which is considered legally drunk!

People sleeping four hours a night were found falling asleep during the cognitive tests at the lab.

Ironically, sleep-deprived individuals are often unaware that they are not getting enough sleep. Due to the body's inclination to adapt, as people get less sleep, their demand of sleep becomes lower. The concept works in-sync with that of a drunk man who claims he is not drunk.

If you think of this in a larger context, this is an incredibly serious issue. One study found that hospital interns working 24 hours were 61 percent more likely to stab themselves with a needle or scalpel. Recognizing the serious detriments of sleep deprivation, hospitals worldwide have finally started to change their work hours for doctors.

Meanwhile, the American Automobile Association has stated that drowsy driving causes 1 in 5 fatal crashes in the U.S. In fact, a new report from the National Highway Traffic Safety Administration estimated that drowsy driving results in 1.2 million collisions every year, causing around 8,000 deaths per year. To combat such casualties, agencies have pushed states to make laws that punish drivers who fall asleep while driving. Some automakers like Mercedes-Benz and Ford have developed technology that can read your steering habits and detect when you are getting drowsy.

As long as the sleep deprivation in our society continues, self-driving cars may by the only solution to this problem. In recent years, companies like Uber, Google, and Tesla have attempted to develop self-driving cars. It seems, however, that we won't be able to place all our eggs on one basket. In March, Uber suspended its self-driving program due to a vehicle crash in Arizona, suggesting that cars still require considerable human intervention.

If people cannot perform a task as simple as driving due to sleep deprivation, imagine what type of impact sleep deprivation has on our ability to make decisions and judgments as well as our ability to absorb information and solve problems.

THE SLEEP CHALLENGE: OUR BIOLOGICAL LIMITATION

Beyond all this information, the most important facts about sleep deprivation are those regarding its effect on death. Studies consistently find that people with less than 7-8 hours of sleep each day have a 12 percent increase in the likelihood of death. Unfortunately, that is true even for people whose sleep is inhibited by sleep disorders.

University of Wisconsin-Madison researchers found that over the course of an 18-year study, people with severe, untreated sleep apnea had triple the death rate of those without it. For participants who had 30 or more breathing pauses per hour while asleep, their risk of cardiovascular death was five times greater than that of those who had fewer than five pauses. In a different study from the American Academy of Sleep Medicine, people with moderate to severe obstructive sleep apnea (the most common form of the condition) were four times more likely to die and three times more likely to die from cancer. They also more than doubled their risk of developing cancer and were nearly four times more likely to have a stroke.

In order to ensure that you are sleeping your best, you must regularly monitor yourself. One of the best ways to monitor your sleep is to ask someone if you snore, as snoring can be an important indicator of allergies and obesity (although it may be caused by genetics or even muscle-relaxing medications). Snoring can also be a sign of sleep apnea. Make sure to take such signs seriously.

While science proves again and again that adults who sleep 6-8 hours every day tend to live longer, there are those who are curious about what would happen if we gave up sleep altogether. Like Edison suggested, what would happen if we eliminated sleep from our lives? Luckily, there is a YouTube channel called ASAP Science that explains the process in great detail. Apparently, when you first enter a sleep-deprived state, you release dopamine which might actually make you feel more energized and positive and increase your sex drive

— things that actually sound appealing.

However, the good news stops there. During that time, your brain also starts to shut off the regions that control your decision-making. This reduces perception, cognition, and your body's ability to react to stimuli and increases impulsive behaviors.

After two days without sleep, your immune system shuts down. Three days of sleep deprivation sometimes leads people to hallucination.

You might find it interesting that the longest study of sleep-deprived individuals to date was 11 days long, and it ended when researchers began to fear that the participants would suffer irreparable damages. Luckily, none of the participants displayed any long-term medical, physiological, neurological, or psychiatric problems.

On the other hand, a study by Allan Rechtschaffen at the University of Chicago showed that rats could only last about two weeks without sleep, although he couldn't figure out if they were dying from the lack of sleep or the constant stress of being woken up.

While we have no studies showing that death results directly from lack of sleep, there is a sleep disorder whose symptoms closely resemble this situation. Fatal Familial Insomnia, a disorder that progressively develops into insomnia, slowly sleep deprives individuals until their organs start to break down from lack of sleep. They often die after around 18 months with the disorder. Currently, only about 100 people around the world are known to have the mutated protein that initiates this sleep disorder. As there is no cure for this disease yet, we are hoping our sleep research will help everyone get better sleep.

During the spring semester of my first year, one of my friends in my program had to juggle an overloaded schedule. With Chinese, a full-time internship, a thesis to write, and four other classes, her schedule did not allow her to sleep more than five hours every day.

At a certain point in her semester, she would wake up every morning to get to work by 7 a.m., work until 4 p.m., then walk over two miles to get to school for a 2.5-hour class. Once she got home, she would only have time to sleep for about four hours before she had to repeat the schedule. She told me that she followed this schedule for two months straight.

One day, she unexpectedly had a seizure inside her cubicle. Alarmed and caught off guard, the people working around her called the ER, but by the time they arrived, she refused to sign the papers to get on the ambulance because she was worried that going to the hospital would set her back in her schedule.

Since then, my friend has told me that she has not only reduced her course load by half but also has decided against an internship for her last semester. While she used to never take naps, she has come to enjoy them more frequently.

Like my friend's experience, there are often times in our lives when our schedules give us no room to think. Our only drive is to move forward. However, during those times, it is worth taking a step back to think if everything you are working for is really worth it. Once my mother presented me with a great analogy. She said, "If money is an integer '0,' relationships is another zero, and maybe family is two zeros, health is the only integer that is a '1.'"

Initially confused, I asked her what she meant.

She explained that when you are writing a 10,000, for example, the four zeros add up to nothing without the first integer, "1." She continued, "Without health, everything else in life is meaningless."

She is right. There is nothing quite better than being healthy. Without sleep, you are forgoing your health. It will show in your skin, your personality, and your performance. So go to bed. Yes, right now — even if it's for a short catnap.

Chapter Summary:

- Sleep makes you look better, which means that you are more competitive in the workplace.
- Driving while sleep-deprived is as bad as drunk driving!
- Sleep can change your personality, hindering you to being your true self.

CHAPTER 3

THE SLEEPING SAMURAI AND THE DORMANT DRAGON

———

During their eighth match, the samurai and dragon noticed that their bodies were moving faster and with more power than they were during the first. They were lasting longer in their matches. Regardless, their matches always ended in a draw.

As always, they ended with a promise for a rematch.

This time, however, the dragon complimented the samurai, "You put up a good fight for a human."

The samurai replied, "You do well for a creature without discipline and drive."

And they laughed. That evening, they did not immediately return home. Like the many afternoons they had spent napping together, they talked to each other, lulling each other to sleep.

The samurai told the dragon, "I'll let you in on a little secret. I have been spending less time on my drills recently because our fights have been so exhausting. The first thing I do is go to sleep when I get back home."

The dragon hissed back, "I no longer have the energy to admire my shadows each night after our battles."

With the bright stars and moonlight glistening in the sky, they fell asleep together until the rays of the sun woke them up in the morning.

For many years, the samurai and the dragon battled ferociously. Their daily battles became a routine. Animals in the forest would come to see their daily matches to admire their beauty.

Meanwhile, back in their respective cottage and cave, the samurai and dragon perfected their sleeping schedules. The samurai would grind his blade to use the next day as if he was meditating. Breathing in and out slowly, he could fall asleep in seconds, *always waking up to the first sun rays entering his home. The dragon would come back to his cave in one mighty sweep. In just two turns, he would assemble himself into a perfect sphere.*

In the morning, the samurai would practice his daily drill while the dragon would make his rounds of the forest. Then, they would meet at their daily napping spot. The samurai would lean against the dragon, and they'd take their daily nap. They would wake up at the same hour, when the samurai would practice his drill one more time while the dragon made his rounds of the forest one more time.

Soon, they would be ready for another fight.

**

Why do you sleep?

If the main point is not when you sleep but how much you sleep, you may wonder why that is. What often goes unnoticed is the fact that sleep works under homeostasis, a state of equilibrium or balance.

Scientists have named the intuitive process of returning to one state due to excess of the other "sleep pressure," often regulated by our circadian rhythm and daylight in addition to other internal and external factors.

While scientists are unsure why we have developed this homeostasis in our biological systems, they have developed a number of theories to try and explain it. The main four are as follows: 1) Inactivity helped our ancestors survive because they would hide quietly and go unnoticed by predators, 2) lowering metabolism rates during our sleep saves the amount of energy we spend throughout the day, 3) sleep restores the resources we expend during the day, and 4) sleep occurs for the healthy maintenance of the brain. While these theories have been contentiously debated in scientific communities, it is uncertain if we will ever find the reason why we sleep the way we do. What is certain, however, is that sleep is associated with memory, ability to learn, and brain development as well as appetite, immune system, and aging.

A HISTORICAL NEED FOR SLEEP

Throughout history, there have been times when people were deprived of the amount of sleep necessary to maintain homeostasis. With the Industrial Revolution starting around the 1760s in Great Britain, people started to work in factories to mass-produce items. With little protection for the workers, factories started to demand more labor, lengthening work hours for little pay. While injuries were common during this time, there was no guaranteed insurance for workers whose fingers were cut off, who suffered mild burns, or who had parts of their bodies amputated.

Around the start of the 19th century, various measures were being formed to protect the workers. A large part of the debate was the argument that workers needed to work less and sleep more. In 1819, the Cotton Mills and Factories Act outlawed the employment of children younger than nine and limited children ages nine to 16 to working 12 hours per day, arguing that they would be less likely to fall asleep, get injured, or receive beatings from supervisors. By 1833, this number was reduced to 48 hours per week and included two hours of schooling.

For adults, the Factories Act of 1844 had women and young adults working 12-hour days while requiring that masters and owners be held accountable for the injuries of their workers. The Factories Act of 1847, known as the 10-hour bill, also limited working hours for women and young people to 10 hours per day with a maximum of 63 hours per week. This eventually culminated in the Factory Acts of 1850 and 1856, which simply stated that factories could not dictate the work hours for women and children. They limited all work hours to between 6 a.m. and 6 p.m. in the summer and between 7 a.m. and 7 p.m. during the winter.

While these laws probably passed because the effects of sleep deprivation were already clear, in 1913, various studies were published that found a correlation between working hours and number of accidents, suggesting that sleep deprivation increased the possibility of workplace-related injuries and other health detriments.

THE SECRET WEAPON OF WORLD ATHLETES, MUSICIANS, AND INVENTORS

Now that we have seen how people have been deprived of sleep throughout history (and the negative consequences that have ensued), let's delve into what happens when we sleep more. Recently, many researchers have studied how sleep enhances athletes' performance. Since professional athletes must remain in top shape to perform well, they are often considered the paragon of health.

In 2011, Cheri Mah published a study following 11 members of the Stanford basketball team with sleep sensors for two weeks. Finding that they averaged about six-and-a-half hours of sleep each night, she told them to aim for a minimum of 10 hours each night. Once the players' average rose up to eight-and-a-half hours per night, their performance improved dramatically while their fatigue levels dropped. For example, sprint times were .7 seconds faster, free-throw shooting rose by nine percent, and three-point shots increased by 9.2 percent.

Olympians sleep for about eight hours a day with a half-hour nap each day. Michael Phelps has said, "Eat, sleep, and swim, that's all I can do." Meanwhile, famous Swedish tennis player Roger Federer has said, "If I don't sleep 11-12 hours a day, it's not right." This is no surprise, considering how tennis players can increase their hitting accuracy by 42 percent simply by getting enough sleep. Additionally, sleep improves split-second decision-making ability by 4.3 percent. For swimmers, sleep extensions can improve reaction time by 17 percent. Imagine what a difference that can make in a 50-meter freestyle race!

If you aren't an athlete, perhaps you are a musician who is in need of more artistic genius. K. Anders Ericsson followed the lives of expert violinists to find, as expected, that the main things they did each day were practice and sleep. However, a key finding in the report was that they sleep more than the average person. He found that the best violinists slept about 8.6 hours per day, while their teachers slept 7.8 hours per day. Additionally, the best violinists took the most naps, averaging 2.8 hours per week. What is even more surprising is that this already seemed to be common knowledge among violinists, as they rated sleep as "highly relevant for improvement of violin performance."

It is therefore not surprising that many musicians have taken advantage of sleep to improve their musical abilities. However, not all musicians aim to solidify their performance skills through long sleep and naps. Some musicians acquire their inspirations through dreams. Take Paul McCartney, for instance, who admitted that the concept for "Yesterday" came to him in a dream when he heard a classical string ensemble playing the melody. As soon as he woke up, he sat in front of his upright piano next to his bed and copied what he heard from his dream onto his paper. Initially, he was worried that he had heard the song elsewhere and dreamt up a repetition of an already-existing song.

In the movie *Inception*, a professional thief played by Leonardo DiCaprio makes a living by stealing information from other people's subconscious. In the film, he is offered a chance to erase his criminal record if he implants another person's subconscious into a target's subconscious. The idea that we can utilize our subconscious in our daily lives is an incredibly appealing concept for musicians and other artists. It's definitely another reason to increase your sleep and nap time while leaving your notebook (or piano) next to your bed.

Even apart from athletics and music, some research suggests that sleep can help with all kinds of interests and hobbies. One study found that professional Tetris players who dreamt the most about Tetris improved their performance faster than those who claimed that they didn't dream about Tetris, even though the amount of hours they practiced the game were similar.

Over the years, scientists have come to theorize about the power of dreams. Before the 1950s, scientists assumed that the brain shuts down during sleep. In the same way that computers reboot to function on a clean slate, Harvard psychologist Deirdre Barrett believes that dreams provide a space for people to work out problems where they can use visual analysis and out-of-the-box thinking.

It is therefore not surprising that some notable figures in history have attributed their success to their dreams. For example, Elias Howe invented the sewing machine after he had a nightmare about cannibals using spears that resembled needles. The image imprinted in his brain during his dream soon made him a multimillionaire as the inventor of a product that would revolutionize the world. In 2004, his name was placed in the U.S. National Inventors Hall of Fame.

Another dream that drastically changed the world was that of Friedrich Kekule, who sketched up a drawing of the dancing atoms he had seen in his dream. In another nap, he saw a serpent twisted into a circle and biting its own tail, helping him realize that benzene was structured similarly and thus changing the field of organic chemistry.

While our society continues to underestimate the value of sleep, many individuals in the world who bypassed or overcame the stigma have attained incredible success through their sleep. Throughout my lifetime, I have also heard my peers talking about how some people would listen to an audiobook or classical music to study or prepare for their music recital. There was a time when my sister had a dream diary after reading a book about how successful people utilized them to achieve their success. Among the world's top athletes, violinists, and Tetris players, there are avid sleep lovers who show that sleep is not your enemy but your friend, helping you in often unplanned, incalculable ways.

THE SLEEPING SAMURAI AND THE DORMANT DRAGON

As discussed in the first chapter, our current society has an unhealthy stigma against sleep. CEOs and world leaders already buy into the argument that less sleep is better. Take Donald Trump, for instance, who has regularly claimed that he sleeps less than four hours per night. Like Edison, such leaders often forget to mention that they also take power naps regularly. In recent years, however, some entrepreneurs have stepped up and admitted that their generous sleep schedules are the source of their success. But what do they do differently? Who are the samurai and dragons in our society?

One of the most famous and ongoing leaders of sleep in the world of entrepreneurship has been Amazon CEO Jeff Bezos. In an interview with Thrive Global, Bezos explained that the productive couple of hours that you get from shortchanging your sleep is an illusion. "When you're talking about decisions and interactions, quality is usually more important than quantity," he says.

Unlike Jeff Bezos who has regularly advocated for a healthy sleep schedule from the very beginning, entrepreneur and CEO of GreenPal Bryan Clayton admitted that there was a time when he used to get out of bed between 4 and 5 a.m. in hopes of being more productive. However, through experience, he found that he was only half as effective compared to when he would get eight or nine hours of sleep.

On the other hand, multimillionaire and president of Celebri-Ducks and Cocoa Canard Craig Wolfe says, "I actually get up between 8:15 and 9 a.m., but since I manufacture in different time zones, I usually have to work into the night." For Wolfe, being successful isn't about the when you start and end work but about setting up time throughout the day when you are 100 percent available to meet your day-to-day business needs.

He explains, "For instance, I may sleep in, but when 9 a.m. comes, I am taking calls no matter what. To be most efficient, I have set blocks of time when I work on proposals, when I return calls, and when I do public relations."

To accomplish his daily tasks, Wolfe schedules his time to maximize his efficiency, even if that means that he needs to block off time in the evening when other people are resting to devote time to his factory overseas. "You can be a late riser, but you better be a master of setting priorities and being disciplined with how you schedule your time each day and night."

Some other entrepreneurs are more savvy planning their sleep around their work. Paul Koger, a self-employed millionaire trader and owner of Foxytrades, regularly gets up at 9:15 a.m., just 15 minutes before the markets open. He advises that if you like to sleep in, you can be successful if you tackle more difficult tasks when you are more productive and take it easy in the morning.

Natasha Nelson, owner of Kauzbots, has a similar strategy where she focuses on scheduling high-value activities by organizing her schedule the night before. "I plan out my next morning as the last thing I do at the end of my workday," says Nelson. "I don't have to take time to get organized and start making my to-do list that morning. Since I do get emails and texts in the evening that are unavoidable, I always add them to my to-do list that I look at immediately when I wake up. There is no lapse in time from getting out of bed and work starting, and I don't have to spend a half-hour or so getting my day organized." As a multimillionaire who has had experience selling her Yogurtini business to the Rocky Mountain Chocolate Factory, she wakes up between 8 and 9 a.m. regularly.

Meanwhile, Brittani Nelson is a millionaire "business matchmaker" who wakes up at 8 a.m. to block off her entire day

— from tasks to sales, follow-up to marketing, and more — making sure to balance current clients and new client activity so that her pipeline remains full. She also is disciplined about secret time-wasters. She says, "I avoid logging onto Facebook or social media unless it is my scheduled time for marketing online. I avoid checking emails and phone calls I am not expecting until it is time to check email and return phone calls."

Nelson also understands what works best for her. Instead of using Google Calendar, apps, or other devices, she still uses her paper worksheet to plan out her schedule. For her, being successful means having the right systems in place to make the most out of your time, regardless of what time of day the clock says.

In a world where innovation is becoming the key to success, the malleability of our sleeping schedule may come to us as a blessing and a curse. In a world where we have more research, more technology, and more innovation related to sleep, our job is to figure out how to utilize them in a way that benefits our health and professional success.

COLLEGE LIFE: THE EARLY BIRDS VS. THE NIGHT OWLS

To this day, I have trouble falling asleep at night. Although my sleep schedule changes with the seasons, I've noticed that my ideal sleeping hours during my school vacations have been 1 a.m. to 9 a.m. There was a time when I thought that my sleeping schedule was a phase. Various research shows that children and teenagers have hormones that not only push them to sleep more but later during the night. However, like my mother, even on days that I had nothing to do, I soon found myself reading, watching television, and looking for other activities to fill up the time late at night as I waited for bedtime to come. If I had to categorize myself, I would call myself a "night owl."

In recent years, some research has suggested that late sleepers are actually more intelligent, to night owls' delight. According to *Psychology Today*, virtually all species follow a circadian rhythm that dictates one's cycle of sleep and wakefulness. However, for humans who have had the opportunity to "evolve" from artificial lighting, those who are more "nocturnal" may also be more intelligent. In *STUDY* Magazine, psychologist Satoshi Kanazawa from the London School of Economics and Political Science collected a large sample of young Americans and found that intelligent children with an IQ over 125 were much more likely to grow into nocturnal adults who would go to bed past midnight (12:29 a.m.), as opposed to children with an IQ less than 75, who would go to bed around 11:41 p.m. Following his research, *Elite Daily* suggested that those who sleep late tend to be anti-establishment, more open-minded, and more proactive.

While I accept most of the information from these articles with open arms, some of my other research on sleep questions its validity. According to one ASAP Science video, people are naturally born with different sleeping cycles. Biologically, it was probably beneficial for people to be born with different sleep schedules so that groups could keep awake to guard themselves. From their research, they found that night owls tend to have less white matter inside the brain, which means that there are less pathways for feel-good hormones like serotonin and dopamine. Due to their heightened levels of cortisol — also known as the "brave" hormone — night owls are likely to be more creative and have higher cognitive abilities. Further research has suggested that the lack of white matter inside night owls' brains increases their proclivity for risk-taking behavior.

Whether you are a morning lark or a night owl, one thing does not change: Everyone needs sleep. What these students or people need is the ability to change their schedules in ways that will maximize their productivity levels. College is one of the best places for students to start experimenting with their sleep schedules, although as Huffington writes, "What makes getting sleep in college much harder is the fear of missing out."

Most colleges have a starting time of 8 a.m., but experts like Jonathan Kelly who advises NPR Ed think that 10 or 11 a.m. would be a better starting time for students. Kelly's research found that up to 83 percent of students could improve their performance if colleges allowed students to choose their own ideal start time in a regular six-hour day. Studies have found that ample sleep can also affect self-esteem and confidence. In 2015, the Japanese Ministry of Education had its first sleep survey which found that 46 percent of the students who slept between 9 and 10 p.m. said that they "somewhat like who they are," while that percentage dropped to 30 percent for students sleeping between 1 and 2 a.m.

During college, one friend told me that she had shifted her entire schedule three hours behind since her classes started in the afternoon. As she headed out to breakfast at 10 a.m. every morning, her day sounded like a typical high school student's day with a bedtime that came around 2 a.m. My friend was a wise sleep goddess. She knew how to control her own sleep schedule.

You can do it, too! Don't fight your sleep schedule!

In spite of our history and research, sleep deprivation continues in the workplace. While the reasons why we sleep are still unclear, it is clear that we need sleep to function. While people thrive under different sleeping conditions and hours, athletes, musicians, and inventors all learn to harness the power of sleep to perform their best. It seems to me that Thomas Edison, in spite of his problematic statements about sleep, brought us an enormous tool for productivity: The lightbulb has allowed us to change our schedules in ways that better suit us for our ideal circadian rhythm.

It is now time to strategize your sleep in a world where sleep is seen as a weakness!

It doesn't matter whether you are a morning lark or a night owl. Just remember that not all sleep is equal. Students and working professionals should work to sleep in bed at least 85 percent of the time every day, falling asleep within 30 minutes, waking up no more than once per night, and avoiding getting up within the first 20 minutes of sleep. With this in mind, now it is time for you to become the sleeping samurai and dormant dragon. Add in a nap or two if you have to. It is time to work against the imposed system to awaken your inner genius!

Chapter Summary:

- There is no perfect sleeping schedule in the same way that there isn't a single diet that encompasses the variety of people in the world.
- Sleeping enhances musical and athletic performances. It also does wonders for your brain activity.
- Our world continues to downplay the importance of sleep, and it is your job to fight against it!

CHAPTER 4

INNOVATION IN SLEEP, NAPS, AND HEALTH

The samurai and the dragon were preparing for battle when a mysterious entity appeared in front of them. It was neither human nor a creature of any kind that they had seen before. It was neither light nor darkness.

It spoke, "I am the god of sleep. Both of you have grown incredible power, strength, and beauty through me, but you have never thought to repay me. You have never made a sacrifice, offering me routine dreams with no inspiration of fascination. How will you appease my anger?"

The samurai and dragon realized the gravity of the situation. Suddenly their bodies and minds ached of indescribable pain.

"We apologize for our sin. Please forgive us!" they cried out.

"What will you do to repay my kindness?" the god of sleep asked.

"Anything," they replied.

"Well, in that case, I will take your friendship as a sacrifice. You, samurai, will continue to sleep during the night and work during the day. However, you, dragon, will only be able to sleep during the day and roam throughout the night. You will never again be able to see each other to battle and show off the skills that you've honed with my blessing."

In an instant, the mysterious entity disappeared. The samurai suddenly felt tired and collapsed under the night sky. The dragon, feeling more awake than ever before, suddenly realized that he no longer felt the excruciating pain he had felt just a minute earlier.

Looking sadly at the samurai, he put him on his back and flew him to his cottage. He gently put him down on the grass in front of his door. After taking one last look, he flew away, never looking back.

In the coming years, the samurai and dragon were faithful to the god of sleep. Instead of spending all his days by the cottage going through his daily drills, the samurai would explore the *forest looking for his friend. He often wondered in which cave his dragon friend would spend the mornings. He wondered where he would be flying during the night.*

Meanwhile, the dragon would take time to visit his friend during the night. He would wonder how the samurai would spend his days. He wondered if he was still going through his daily drills. He wondered how strong and agile he had become. The dreams from his imagination fed the god of sleep during the day.

Satisfied with his work, the god of sleep decided to extend the curse of the samurai and dragon to the entire world. All the humans and animals in the universe could no longer choose the hours of their sleep. They could only sleep in the hours that pleased the god of sleep.

While the god of sleep was happy for awhile, it eventually realized that the decision was a mistake. Suddenly, the dreams it received were no longer rich and fruitful. While the dreams of the samurai and dragon continued to feed it incredible strength, all the other dreams it collected became bland. The god of sleep was confused.

**

Imagine waking up to an alarm that forces you to jog every morning. Well, Clocky Alarm is exactly that!

Ranging from $17.99 to $60.35, Clocky Alarms are shaped like smiley faces and have wheels on their sides instead of ears. "Unlike an alarm clock, as soon you hit snooze, Clocky will jump off your nightstand and start wheeling around your bedroom in search of a hiding place," as it is described on the website. "You'll be wide awake before you know what's hit you!" And for the most reluctant wakers among us, there is the Northwest Flying Alarm Clock, which sends a propeller up in the air when the alarm sounds that you need to catch and return to its station to turn the alarm off.

Back when I was in high school and I had not yet discovered the world of innovative sleep products such as the Clocky Alarm clock, I had perfected my own customized technique to ensure that I'd get up on time. In an attempt to prevent shivering in the chilly morning air as I changed out of my pajamas, I would bring the next day's outfit into the warmth of my bed, sealing it off from the frigid outside air. Once the alarm went off, in a half-conscious state, I would slowly dress under the covers into the clothes that had absorbed my body warmth throughout the night. By the time my father would come to my bed, all I had to do was take off the cover, put on my shoes, and carry my bag outside!

As helpful as the routine was, I needed a more sustainable practice. I now know that there are innovations that would have alleviated some of my struggles. In recent years, the global sleep industry has been expanding at an unprecedented rate, introducing sleep aid products that range from small products like the ostrich pillow — a large, plush hood that can serve as a comfortable headrest anywhere — to mega-technology nap pods. The world has entered the largest sleep revolution since Thomas Edison invented the lightbulb. This chapter will cover the latest sleep innovation offerings in the market and how these various tools can help us get better-quality sleep.

NECK RESTS, VIETNAMESE COFFEE, AND RED BULL

Throughout my college years, I traveled far and wide. The summer after my freshman year, I traveled abroad for the first time to Chile. The following winter, I went to South Korea for the first time. Then came Mexico. Before graduating, I had made a total of six trips abroad.

What I learned from these trips was that "traveling" was the worst part of traveling. While I loved exploring new cities, tasting new cuisines, and meeting new people, oftentimes the long, cold flights would leave me achy, tired, and sleep-deprived. I found that even in cases where I had technically slept a full eight hours on the flight, I would feel just as exhausted as if I'd had little to no sleep.

Right after graduating from Harvard, my friends and I agreed to travel together to Southeast Asia. It would be my first time in the region. Already having done some research on Japan's nap pods, I toted along some interest in naps and sleep aid products before heading to the trip. However, I had no idea that I would be exposed to so many new wonders during my trip to Thailand, Cambodia, and Vietnam.

During my trip to Cambodia, my friends took me to a silk farm where I got to see the local Cambodians making everything from scarves to neckties and dresses to coin pouches with the silk they produced on the farm. As my friend and I browsed through the items, I felt one of the the neck rests to test the firmness. I immediately fell in love! At the time, I had already been browsing Ostrich Pillows that would allow me to sleep anywhere and any time. But this Cambodian silk neck rest was perfect, with dreamy softness from the silk cover and just the right amount of cotton placed inside to ensure that my neck would remain in place. Over time, I realized that the benefits of neck rests extend beyond the individual naps you can take anywhere and any time. One study found that people with chronic neck pain could relieve their pain more effectively by pairing a neck support pillow to their exercise treatment with a physical therapist.

Although our time in Thailand, Cambodia, and Vietnam spanned only about two weeks, our packed schedule meant that we were aboard either a plane or a train for one-third of the time. This left plenty of time for me to use my neck rest along the way. Throughout the trip, I added a sleep mask and ear plugs, promising me the perfect sleeping experience. For many business travelers, neck rests, sleep masks, and ear plugs are obvious must-have items that take precedence on their packing lists. Some savvy planners might also add comfortable slip-on shoes and a thin, light blanket to their carry-on bag. With a limited college budget, I had to think carefully about whether each item was worth the money. In the end, they all were.

The neck rest wasn't the only thing that stuck with me during my trip to Southeast Asia. So were the various drinks that I had. I am not referring to alcohol, but to energy drinks.

In Thailand, I learned that Red Bull was founded by Chaleo Yoovidhya, a local and ordinary Thai who started his own company, TC Pharmaceuticals. In an attempt to help factory workers and truck drivers stay awake during long shifts, Yoovidhya crafted Krating Daeng-Thai, which was a mixture of sugar, caffeine, and taurine. In 1982, Austrian entrepreneur Dietrich Mateschitz discovered the drink while sitting at a bar in the Mandarine Hotel in Hong Kong and decided to track down Yoovidhya so that they could found Red Bull together.

The drink did not become immediately successful and expanded relatively slowly in the Eastern European markets.

However, once the drink entered the U.S. in 1997, it became an instant success. Since its official launch in Austria in 1987, the company has expanded to 79 countries in 25 years. Today, Red Bull sells over four billion cans annually worldwide.

Funnily enough, I drank Red Bull for the first time during my junior year in college because there was a free promotion for flavored Red Bull. There was a four-pack for every student inside our college dorms, and since more than half of my suitemates didn't drink coffee or energy drinks, I took the liberty of taking their drinks.

My first experience with Red Bull conformed to what the advertisements had promised me. I felt like I was flying "with wings." I had never felt so focused in my life. Unlike the five-hour energy drink that I had tried during my freshmen year, I didn't feel any jitters as I worked through the night. I told my friends that the experience felt "too good," so there was no way that the drink could be good for you. Regardless, I was hooked. On nights when I was writing a paper or studying for an important exam, I would bring out a can of my friends' Red Bull, mumble a brief prayer that I'd be alive the next day, and open the can to start my night.

So, being in the motherland of Red Bull, I felt I had to buy a bottle in memory of my many sleepless nights during college. Instead of buying a can that resembled the ones available in the U.S., I decided to buy the small, rectangular glass bottles. The taste? Unfortunately, it was no different than what I had tasted in the U.S. Yet the different packaging style was enough of a novelty for me. I was satisfied.

While Red Bull was a novelty item I purchased in Thailand, Vietnamese coffee came to me as a surprise. Along the trip, I accidentally ordered the first coffee on the menu on a street in Vietnam thinking that I would get a typical Americano. Nope. Instead, I got a Vietnamese coffee famous for its strong flavor, high caffeine content, and condensed milk. Speaking of coffee, I noticed that there were at least a couple of coffee shops in the busy streets of Hanoi, Ho Chi Minh City, and Hue. Everywhere I walked, I had the opportunity to consume more caffeine, resulting in ongoing jitters for the rest of day. I was quite a happy soul during my entire trip in Southeast Asia.

NEURO SLEEP AND MELATONIN

Now there are plenty of people who believe that energy drinks, coffee, and sleep-aid pills are detriments to sleep. While it's true that these solutions come with certain risks, most times such dangers are overly exaggerated.

Although I have utilized caffeinated and energy drinks more often than sleep-inducing drinks in my life, I once came across a drink called Neuro Sleep, a dietary supplement to help with restful sleep. This drink comes in three flavors: mellow mango, tangerine dream, and peach apricot. Founded in 2009, Neuro Sleep is one of various Neuro health drinks all with specified purposes for your body, including "Reducing Stress" and "Energy Refreshing." A single bottle is around $2 while a 12-pack is usually between $20 and $30, making the drink relatively cheap. The main ingredient inside Neuro Sleep is melatonin with L-Theanine, which helps relax your body. Online, people have claimed it works. After drinking it, I was knocked out as well.

Later, I learned that the reason why the drink has been so effective is the melatonin inside. Melatonin is a hormone that our body produces naturally at night as it gets darker. Its levels usually start rising around 8 p.m. before peaking at 3 a.m., when your body temperature happens to be at its lowest. Around 1994, MIT neuroscientist Dr. Richard Wurtman introduced melatonin after patenting the supplement in hopes of curing insomnia in older populations. Although he warned that people shouldn't self-medicate themselves with melatonin, the pills soon came to the market labeled as "inexpensive, easily accessible, naturally occurring and considered safe."

In an attempt to learn more about melatonin, I experimented with the pills myself. Once again, I knocked myself out.

However, the magic also had its flaws. Even after a long, eight-hour sleep, I found myself groggy and tired, waking up with a numbing headache. Not surprisingly, the use of melatonin has been hotly debated in both the scientific and larger community. At the end of the day, melatonin is a great way to induce sleep, but doesn't necessarily maintain sleep, making it perfect for jet lag or adjusting to changing shifts in the workplace.

While there still isn't enough evidence to prove the potential side effects of melatonin, it is surprising to know that the melatonin we buy in stores is 10 times the recommended amount. In 2001, MIT concluded that the correct dosage for melatonin was between .3 and 1 mg. The overdosage is surprising because research shows that people with excess melatonin often enter a state of overwhelming drowsiness. While there isn't enough data yet to confirm that overdoses of melatonin will negatively impact your health, desensitizing yourself from any drug does not sound like the best idea.

In recent years, I have tried breaking the small melatonin pills in half, and it has worked wonders. I not only fall asleep more quickly but also wake up on time without feeling as groggy (I won't lie, however, I still feel a bit more tired than I do when I sleep naturally.). For those of you who need a quick adjustment in your sleep schedule, you may want to consult a doctor before purchasing some over-the-counter melatonin pills.

THE SLEEP MARKET

After a year of self-debating, I finally purchased my own "Suitsy" from Betabrand.

In case you're wondering what a Suitsy is, it is a onesie that looks like a suit so that you can comfortably lounge in your office space while looking professional. In 2014, creator Jesse Herzog partnered with Betabrand to make a onesie that could serve as loungewear, sleepwear, and professional attire. The results were quite impressive. But it's not cheap, with a price tag of $378.

Since buying the Suitsy, I have worn it in D.C. for various events including conferences, happy hours, social gatherings, and work. Funnily enough, not only were people convinced that it was a typical suit, they complimented the suit asking where I got the jacket or where I got the shirt. Sheepishly, I would explain my little secret to them.

In the years that followed, the advertisements that appeared in my Amazon purchase recommendations were related to innovative sleep technology. Among them were Ostrich Pillows, which cover your head so you can rest it on flat surfaces, — like desks — comfortably while you take a nap. In addition to the opening for your head, the Ostrich Pillow has two openings on top for your hands.

There is no doubt that the Ostrich Pillow sounds awesome, except it's really bulky and ugly. If you put one on, you closely resemble an alien without eyes. While the concept of the product was appealing, I could not get myself to actually purchase the item in fear that it would draw too much attention and ridicule. Today, I am still debating whether I should get an Ostrich Pillow, which costs about $30 on Amazon. Even beyond the aesthetic, the bulkiness would make it cumbersome to carry around.

As you can tell, I have become very invested in buying products related to sleep and productivity. To this day, I continue to research products already out in the market that might help me sleep anywhere or any time I need to so that I can be productive when I need to be. Luckily, the market has already caught on. In the same way that Trader Joe's and Whole Foods have expanded with a growing customer base interested in green, healthy food options, there is a growing number of customers wanting to find products that will help them master their sleep.

Between the years 2016 and 2022, the global sleep industry is expected to grow 6.3 percent each year. That means that the market is expected to grow by $30 million within seven years! This market includes innovative products like mattresses, pillows, and anti-snoring strips. Meanwhile, the issue of sleep deprivation has been growing worldwide, especially among the world's most developed countries. According to the RAND Corporation, the U.S. has been losing 2.28 percent of the GDP every year due to sleep loss, totaling $411 billion every year!

As previously mentioned, however, we have seen the most progress in Asia. As Japan and South Korea are currently the two most sleep-deprived countries in the world, they have also been the frontrunners in the napping industry. Take 3rd Seat, for instance, a place where customers are offered one of 15 booths for napping. While sitting there, you can also order a lunch for less than $10. Unfortunately for customers, the seats are so popular that they are nearly always full.

Meanwhile, Goku no Kimochi or "scalp massage" offers a "head spa" with the intention of getting their customers to sleep. Based in Tokyo and Osake, hour-long spa Goku no Kimochi costs 5,700 yen to 6,200 yen (approximately $57 to $62). Some customers have claimed that the head spa helps with sleep for subsequent nights after the massage. As they are so popular, the massages are fully booked and require customers to reserve them three months in advance. If that is not enough, there are Remm hotel chains like Hankyu Hanshin Hotels — located in Tokyo, Osaka, and Kagoshima — that attempt to help customers go to sleep immediately after they finish their day. The rooms' beds feature mattresses with extra springs. The single rooms have no bathtubs. Instead, a shower booth is separated from the rest of the room by a glass wall to "make these rooms feel large and more comfortable," a company spokesperson said.

Meanwhile, Japan has also been leading the production of napping devices. For example, a product called "2breathe" functions as a belt that syncs to a smartphone app. It was introduced in March 2016 by Nemulog, a leading textiles maker from the Tokyo-based subsidiary of Teijin. The belt, which sells for about $130, helps users to breathe in a way that encourages them to become drowsy. As the sensor detects the pace of the user's breathing, the app produces a tone through the user's smartphone to induce them to sleep. Apparently, the device is so high-tech that the tone is repeated at just the right interval, prodding the user into prolonged exhalations. While I have never had the opportunity to try the machine myself, it's definitely a novel product that I would like to try in the near future.

Another device from Japan is Omron Healthcare's SleepDesign Navi HSL-003T. Placed near the pillow, this device also works in sync with a smartphone app. Paying particular attention to movement, it not only records the number of times that one tosses and turns but also detects and records the time the body falls asleep. The cost of the device is about $6.

The U.S. has also been developing various devices to measure sleeping patterns, such as the BodyMedia Fit, Fitbit Flex,

Jawbone Up, Basis Band, Innovative Sleep Solutions Sleep Tracker, and Zeo Sleep Manager. However, professors Jeon Lee and Joseph Fink from Johns Hopkins University School of Medicine have expressed that while wearable sleep trackers were collecting immense amounts of information related to individual sleeping habits, they didn't provide enough information to make an educated recommendation for an individual. This is because each device has a different measure of sleep. Without a standardized system to analyze the data, no company could amass enough data to provide individualized attention to the sleep-deprived. If there is a way to collect all the data from the individual companies in a standard form, there is room for incredible growth in sleep research.

NAP PODS

Initially started in Japan, the nap pod industry has been rapidly growing in South Korea, Vietnam, and even Dubai. Usually placed in airports, companies have developed various models to fit the needs of their customers. Ranging from circular designs to rectangular ones, the models have come in the shape of chairs, hammocks, and small rooms.

Their growth has already impacted the U.S. market as well. In San Francisco, DozeSF has been offering a 25-minute nap for $20. Located inside the 12th floor of the beautiful and historic Hobart Building with a marble and brass interior, DozeSF started without venture capital or angel investors.

Meanwhile, companies like Google have used nap pod chairs and renamed them "energy pods." Additionally, both Zappos and Pricewaterhouse Coopers (PWC) have adopted nap pods in their offices. The fact that such big-name corporations are utilizing nap pods serves as a testament to the changing work environment culture that is more receptive to employers' needs and the growing understanding that giving napping perks in the workplace can ultimately increase productivity! So nap on!

Whether it's a six-minute nap or a full 90-minute one, sleep research suggests that napping is the best way to alleviate your ongoing sleep deprivation, outperforming your daily dose of coffee or tea. While this may sound obvious, we rarely put this into practice because of the stigma associated with sleeping. Most companies do not allow spaces to nap. While they offer lunch time, they do not allow workers to take time off during the day to take a quick power nap. In fact, even you may be reading this book and still be thinking that offering napping time in the workplace is a silly idea.

Silly as it may sound, there is no doubt that offering naps in the workplace would increase not only productivity but also the general well-being of workers. Only once we as a society accept that sleep is a natural and important part of our daily biological functions can we harness the true power of sleep.

The art of napping is the future for a more prosperous and productive world.

THE POTENTIAL AND LIMITATIONS OF SLEEP INVENTIONS

In a meeting with one of my mentors, he once mentioned that life is like surfing where you are hunting for the best waves to ride. Out on the vast ocean, you notice where the pillowing waters are highest. Today, the napping industry is one of those waves. We are finding that workers — both young and old — living in dense cities all have a stake in encouraging this new market.

Today, sleeping is not confined to a quiet, secluded bed. Although everyone knows that a dark, cool, and quiet bed is ideal, it is not accessible to everyone. Even those who can access one might not have access to it all the time due to the growing number of jobs that require travel. We cannot expect everyone to follow the "perfect sleep regimen," as it might not even exist. Instead, we have adapted to the lightbulb, mattresses, and pillows that have changed our relationship with sleep.

Contrary to other books that suggest that we must return to an older form of "sleep" from our primitive roots, this chapter focuses on how innovation has been changing and even improving our relationship with sleep.

While technology has seemed to deteriorate the quality of sleep over the years, ongoing innovation in the sleep industry promises us incredible solutions to our growing problems in the modern world. Such sleep innovation technology should be embraced, not avoided, if we are to solve the growing sleep deprivation problem in our society. Embracing change is difficult, but one should not shy away from it because such challenges offer us a better future. In the same way that innovation in the food industry has expanded our vegetarian, vegan, and gluten-free options, the sleep industry offers varied experiences customized to all types of individuals.

The fact that we did not have trains, cars, or airplanes in the past does not mean that we want to live a life without such technology. In fact, in recent years, we have come to take these innovations and increase our use of them. Here are two examples of innovations that have proved to be different than our expectations:

The first is the invention of the car. In New York City, horse-drawn carriages — the main source of local transportation at the time — were causing incredible environmental concerns. Locals believed that in a couple decades, the city would be overrun with horse dung, resulting in an unlivable ghost city. With the invention of Ford's cars, that reality changed.

Although we had formed more invisible and perhaps more dangerous environmental concerns from the carbon dioxide/methane, the innovation has also had unexpected positive results.

The second is the invention of escalators. At the time of this innovation, people believed that escalators would increase productivity as people would climb up the moving stairs and reduce the time it would take to move from floor to floor. The result was mixed. In fact, most people used the invention as an excuse to slow down, often standing still on the escalators.

What we can expect after seeing the various products related to sleep is innovation that will continue to confuse, surprise, and impress us. People will always be sleep-deprived in the same way that they will always be hungry. However, it seems that the sleep market has a long way to go to reach the market size of the food industry. It is a whole new market that has been left untapped. In the same way that the U.S. did not give up on our rocket launch to the moon, sleep innovation must go on.

Chapter Summary:

- There are various inventions that can increase the quality and quantity of naps and sleep in your busy schedule.
- You can control the hours of your sleep and the quality of your

sleep if you strategically use the various innovations related to sleep; these include melatonin and energy drinks.
- Don't accept your sleep schedule passively. Take control of your own sleep by accepting that it is our biological necessity. Work with sleep, not against it!

CHAPTER 5

THE EMERGING SLEEP AND NAPPING INDUSTRY

The god of sleep decided to make its rounds of the forest to see why his dreams were no longer tasteful. It went to the rabbits, owls, grasshoppers, and frogs and asked why they were no longer dreaming. They did not know.

Then, the god of sleep went to a nearby cottage, quietly transformed into a villager, and asked the humans what they were dreaming about. They all replied that they had forgotten how to dream.

The god of sleep was shaken. It could not figure out what had gone wrong. The only thing it had done was separate the samurai and dragon who had been unfaithful to their duty: They had taken advantage of the god of sleep without repaying it for its kindness.

One woman approached the god of sleep and said, "I know why we no longer dream."

"Who are you?" it asked.

The woman replied, "I am a woman, like many villagers here. However, unlike the other women, I have a special gift. I can speak to animals."

"I see. You are a special woman. So what is the reason that the villagers no longer dream?" the god of sleep asked.

"It is because of the samurai and the dragon," said the village woman. "I would often talk to the animals about the samurai and dragon and would hear how the samurai would glisten with sweat as the dragon's scales became covered with dust and soil. Although they fought each other every day, each story was different. The story that the rabbit, owls, grasshoppers, and frogs would relay were all different. Each day, the story they told would be rich and unique."

The god of sleep was still confused.

The village woman continued, "Every day, I would return back *to my people to relay their stories. The husbands and wives, elders, and children would all listen to my story and visualize it. They would then see these images vividly in their heads while dreaming."*

"One day, the animals told me that the samurai and dragon no longer met for battle. Suddenly, the animals did not have any stories to relay. They no longer came to me because they were ashamed that they had no story to share. The animals were sad. I was sad. Soon, the whole village was sad."

Suddenly, the god of sleep understood.

The god of sleep returned to its mysterious form. Looking at the woman, it said, "You are a wise woman. You have taught me something no animal or other human being has been able to explain to me. As a gift, I will provide humans with the ultimate reward: the ability to choose their hours of sleep."

In an instant, the god of sleep disappeared. However, the woman felt different. She felt incredible strength inside her.

**

In April, as I gathered my contacts and research data for this project, more than a couple people messaged me to share a new article by the New York Times, "Sleep is the New Status Symbol." The article covered some of the latest research and innovations related to sleep including nap pods, swimming beds, and screened porches. Meanwhile, Professor Matthew P. Walker at the University of California, Berkeley was studying whether the air quality and other intangibles in our rooms were helping us sleep better.

Some other cool gadgets included a headband with sound waves to help induce people to sleep and Thim, a ring to time your 10-minute nap. What was perhaps the most interesting part of the article was the conception of sleep programs like Sleepio — an online sleep coach — to fight "presenteeism," a new word that was formed to describe the underperforming employees suffering from sleep deprivation.

As mentioned in the previous chapter, the U.S. loses an estimated $411 billion every year from sleep loss. The fight to reduce labor costs is real, and companies are often willing to invest large sums to eventually save costs. What was once the purveyance of old-style mattress and drug companies is now a $32 billion market, embracing the forward thinking of the Silicon Valley.

Accordingly, the purpose of this chapter is two-fold. Its first goal is to help employees get a better understanding of how they can become well-rested and productive members of the workplace. The second is to guide company leaders to make work environments conducive to rest so that companies can profit from more productive employees.

THE POOR AND THE CRAMPED: SLEEP AS A SOCIAL ISSUE

The most sleep-deprived group is often the underprivileged. Consider the unfortunate case of Maria Fernandez, who worked three jobs at three different Dunkin' Donuts in New Jersey. She would often nap inside her car between shifts with her engine running so that she could save time from restarting the car. To ensure that she would never wake up with an empty tank, she kept a container full of fuel in the trunk. On August 25, 2014, the car caught on fire, taking Fernandez's life at the young age of 32.

As you might already imagine, a new study in public health by the University of Pennsylvania has found that Americans are most likely to sacrifice sleep for paid work. The same study found that the 15 percent of Americans working multiple jobs were 61 percent more likely than others to report sleeping six hours or fewer on weekdays.

For many workers, chronic financial instability leads to high levels of anxiety, more time on the roads, and less time taking care of oneself, which often leads to poorer overall health. For many, having a quiet, cool, and dark room to sleep in may be more than they can afford. In a 2006 study by a Croatian medical journal, researchers found that city dwellers living in noisy areas were at a higher risk for sleep disturbances, which led to increased neuroticism, subjective noise sensitivity, and noise annoyance in their daily lives.

Perhaps for this reason, African Americans "were over three times more likely than whites to report very short sleep — less than five hours — while Asians and non-Mexican Hispanics were two to three times as likely." In the previous chapters, we have already discussed the detriments of sleeplessness and the benefits of adequate sleeping and napping. In a land of immigrants, it is ironic to find that many simply don't have the time to sleep the "American Dream."

There are various ways in which societies can change to become more productive. During the early years of South Korea, one of the cultural issues the government aimed to change was how people conceptualized time. Traditionally, South Koreans were notorious for meeting one to two hours past the agreed meeting time. In order to combat this common practice accepted as Korean culture, South Korea initiated a "Time is Gold" campaign. Over time, as Koreans became more punctual, South Korea so completely changed their cultural perception that younger generations oftentimes have no idea the country underwent such a historical change. Subsequently,

South Koreans have acquired the global perception of being hardworking and smart.

Similarly, America is in need of a cultural change. In spite of the fact that the U.S. is one of the most overworked countries in the world, Americans are often stereotyped as fat and lazy. Various studies show that sleep deprivation can lead to both of these realities. While sleeping less at first gives the impression that you are being more productive because you are spending "more" hours working instead of sleeping, your overall productivity decreases when you are exhausted. When you are tired, you are not only less efficient and more sluggish at work but also more likely to overeat. With a slower metabolism from less sleep, you are likely to gain weight, which exacerbates the various negatives linked to sleep deprivation. Sleep deprivation is not an issue that is only rampant in the U.S. but in any city with bustling urban populations. Having lived in various cities ranging from Los Angeles to Seoul and Cambridge to Santiago, I have been able to experience these challenging sleep environments firsthand.

SLEEP AND THE ENVIRONMENT

I still remember my first night in a college dorm as I stared out the windowsill beside my bed. Across the gate, I was faced with a dazzling CVS sign, fervently awakening me with its 24-hour sparkle. A year later, my sister got married and moved from Los Angeles to New York City, "the city that never sleeps."

Although my sister and I grew up in urban Koreatown, Los Angeles, our family home was in a quiet suburban area on a small street, adjacent to homes and apartments. A couple of months in, my sister told me that she was having trouble falling asleep. In New York City, the division between sleeping and socializing was often a single wall, and the hum of the city droned on through the night hours, disrupting her sleep cycle. While this issue might seem like a small conversation that we had in passing, it ended up being a large part of phone conversations, occupying the very time we would normally spend at rest. She would talk about how tired and irritable she felt everyday, and she felt so upset at herself because she did not feel as productive as she used to be.

Embarrassingly, I felt a level of triumph in her statement because my sister had always been an expert sleeper. Unlike me, who might stay up hours praying to fall asleep, my sister could fall asleep within 10 minutes. Now, I wasn't sleeping enough, not only because of the loud noise interrupting my sleep but also because of the invisible pressure building up on college campuses. With a library that was open 24/7 and various locations that students could study any time of the day, I saw my friends up at 2 a.m. with their textbooks open and laptops on. Both my sister and I were facing different pressures for sleep deprivation: external noise and lighting as well as the internal pressures from society.

Today, the issue of urbanization is closely linked to the world's lack-of-sleep epidemic. According to the American Academy of Sleep Medicine, there is an actual term to describe how your environment may be impacting the quality of your sleep: Environmental Sleep Disorder. Neighboring highways, air traffic, loud neighbors, or bright lights that accompany lively city life often make urban areas the worst place to get the sleep you need. And yet, it is only expected that more people will come to live in cities in the future. According to the United Nations, 54 percent of the world's population lives in urban areas today. By 2050, the UN expects that these numbers will increase to 66 percent, surpassing six billion people by 2045. Just to give you some context, in 1950, the urban population was only 746 million.

Environmental deterrents don't just limit sleep; they can limit overall health as well, a concept best visualized by a set of controversial experiments by scientist John Calhoun. In 1947, he ran an experiment with rats to study the effects of overpopulation. After constructing a quarter-acre "rat city" and filling the space with breeding pairs, he hypothesized that the complex would become eventually become home to 5,000 rats as they reproduced. What he found instead was that the population never exceeded 150. Another experiment he ran in 1968 involved eight rats in a "box" called Universe 25.

He observed that the rats became too stressed to reproduce once the rats in the box hit a certain population size. At that point, the rats would act "weirdly, rolling dirt into balls rather than digging normal tunnels. They hissed and fought." Soon enough, all the rats in the box would die.

Throughout his life, Calhoun ran different variations of his experiments, only to find that each carefully constructed "paradise" would collapse. No matter how well the rats were fed and maintained, they would return to a Malthusian nightmare, soon to be termed "The Behavioral Sink." The findings of his experiments immediately caught on in popular media, as people were becoming aware of overpopulation and contemplating whether this rat dystopia could represent the fate of humans. Books like *Soylent Green* and comics like *2000 AD* played on these fears and created a graphic representation of the terrifying future to come.

Today, the validity of the primary findings of his research is debated. Some suggest that while the purported downfall of his living units was an overcrowding problem, in reality, excessive social interaction among rats was the source of their demise. According to Edmund Ramsden in NIH Record, he wrote that rats "who had managed to control space led relatively normal lives," suggesting that humans can cope with overpopulation problems in similar ways.

We are not rats; we are human. Like the smart rats we saw in Calhoun's experiments, we can control space. Considering that we as a society have been able to avoid Malthus's Population Theory — which hypothesized that humans would starve or go into war as we overpopulate because of the increasingly scarce resources available — I also side with the view that we can, in fact, overcome the various problems associated with overpopulation. As humans, we can learn to control our space. Through innovation, we are able to avoid the catastrophic ends suggested by Calhoun's experiments.

Seeing that such innovations are key for our sleep-deprived future, I highlight a couple companies leading such changes.

Equinox health-conscious hotels:

Imagine going to a hotel entirely dedicated to accommodating a healthy lifestyle.

In 2015, Equinox announced its plan to extend their healthy lifestyle brand into hotels. Planning to open their first hotel in 2018 in Manhattan's Hudson Yards, another in Los Angeles in 2019, and several dozens more in the upcoming years, Equinox plans to install gyms on the property open to all hotel guests while also opening the gym to existing gym members.

This venture would make Equinox the first company to expand

their market from the gym industry to the hotel industry, distinguishing itself from other popular brands like Pure Yoga and SoulCycle.

Equinox has one of the highest monthly memberships, costing $230 or more in NYC. In addition to some in Toronto and London, Equinox has more than 80 clubs in the U.S. In a recent interview, Equinox CMO Carlos Becil stated that the new hotels would focus on carefully planning "how you move, nourish, and regenerate your body." He explained that the hotel would allow the clubs to monitor their customers more closely.

The Equinox Hotel will have the largest club that Equinox has ever built at 60,000 square feet, with indoor and outdoor space and pools. In addition to the spa and hotel, Equinox will add office spaces and luxury condos. They are also working to provide a culinary experience that is both healthy and delicious.

Sleepbox and Brooklyn Boulders:

Sleepbox is a company that rents out nap pods. With customizable features, each box has a bed with linen, ventilation system, alarm clock, LCD TV, Wi-Fi, desk space with LED lighting, and electrical outlets for laptops and rechargeables. Additionally, there is cupboard under the bed for your luggage.

In March 2017, Brooklyn Boulders in Somerville, MA installed its first sleepbox in the city for fatigued athletes. With soundproof walls and beds made from foam materials used to make sneaker insoles, these "sleep vending machines" also carry an impressive display of electrical outlets, Wi-Fi, bluetooth-enabled speakers, and a drop-down desk. The sleepbox also offers mood lighting and shades. There are currently three different models to choose from: compact, single, and double.

recharj®:

recharj®, the first company in the D.C. area to offer power nap sessions, has designed a powerful service to a diverse group of sleep-deprived individuals in the area. Recognizing that people want restorative naps, they have utilized their research to offer napping sessions that maximize productivity. The nap sessions in recharj® last only 25-35 minutes so that people do not enter their REM 3 or REM 4 cycles.

recharj® manipulates their music and lighting in a way that they believe will make napping sessions enjoyable and nourishing. Christine Marcella, an integrative psychologist with 20 years of experience in her field, has seen the effect that naps can have on working professionals. Ranging from Uber drivers to working moms and students to young professionals, recharj® has attracted about an equal amount of customers for their napping sessions as their meditative sessions during their soft launch in December 2016.

What people are recognizing, however, is that individual napping sessions can never be easy enough. In the same ways that Uber has revolutionized the way we call our drivers, the napping industry must do the same. Christine has noticed that many workers would cancel their earlier appointments in the day to later times, as their busy schedules often change and their biological needs are often hard to gauge and plan perfectly.

Nestle's Napping Cafes:

Although short-lived, a Japanese café called Nescafe Harajuku collaborated with France Bed in light of World Sleep Day this year to offer customers a chance to nap on a $9,000 bed for free if they purchased at least one food item. On the expensive bed, customers could use their smartphones to set the lights to "relax" mode and a Sony hi-res headphone set to play some white noise so that they could enjoy their two-hour nap. The customers would first be served Nescafe's free decaffeinated coffee before their nap. After their nap, they would be served regular coffee to prepare them to go back to work!

Nestle's napping cafés are a great idea, partially because having coffee before a nap can be a great strategy. How many times have you worried about taking a nap because you knew that you would end up sleeping for hours? When you drink caffeine, it usually takes about 20 minutes to kick in before it starts blocking receptors that transfer adenosine, a chemical compound in your brain that causes drowsiness. With caffeine taking its stead, you get to enjoy the short rejuvenation of the sleep you need but also the effects of the coffee to help you brave through your work!

Conceptualizing Gyms: Status Symbols of Health, Fitness, and Wealth

In the first chapter, I discussed how cultural changes can drastically alter views about trends happening in daily life. In the same way that lightbulbs suddenly brought about a different outlook on sleep, another invention that has changed our views are treadmills that have come to symbolize health, fitness, and wealth. In the 1800s, tread wheels were used to keep British prisoners from idleness. Today, the same machines that developed from torture now account for 40 percent of the fitness equipment industry, worth $3.5 billion in North America in 2015.

Initially, treadmills were used by researchers to study how exercise affected heart and lung disease. In 1968, Kenneth Cooper published a book of his research encouraging readers to improve their cardiovascular fitness. At the time, a large part of the treadmill's success was because before the Industrial Revolution, most people's jobs required physical activity. With the growing number of office jobs, people came to enjoy exercise as a leisure activity. In the 1960s, John F. Kennedy inspired Americans to improve their physical fitness, and a decade later, there was a running boom across the country.

Cooper's book had a lasting impact on American society, as it inspired Bill Staub to launch PaceMaster. His goal was to bring affordable treadmills to every household in the U.S. In the 1980s, he sold 2,000 units per year. By the mid-1990s, he was selling 35,000 a year. In 1991, Life Fitness invented 9500HR, which functioned as a more comfortable treadmill than PaceMaster due to its wide springs and bouncier running surface. In the 1990s and 2000s, treadmills added music and television to appeal to the wider masses.

Today, I see how sleep and naps are being commercialized in the form of power napping centers, health hotels, nap pods, and nap cafes. If you think about it, the development of gyms is a sign of an unlikely cultural shift that proves people are willing to spend money to improve their living. As one of my friends put it, "The world is your running mill. Why pay for it?" During college, many of my friends who simply walked outside with their sneakers on for their runs were still uncomfortable with the idea of running inside a gym.

The fact that people are willing to pay for such services shows a desperate need. People are sleep-deprived. In the same way that torture machines have become exercise machines, these sleep machines — no matter how odd they may seem — are likely to become integrated into our daily lives. Now that you know more about them, be prepared to use them.

They're expected to be available in the markets soon!

Chapter Summary:

- Sleep deprivation is a growing problem in urban areas.
- The sleep and napping industries have been working to solve the problems arising from sleep deprivation.
- In the same way that we learned to use torture machines to keep ourselves fit, we can use seemingly odd innovations to increase our sleep!

CHAPTER 6

BRAVE SLEEP WORLD

Around dusk, the samurai was falling into slumber as the dragon was rising up. Suddenly, they both found themselves at their battleground in front of the god of sleep.

"Both of you are freed from your curse. You are both forgiven. I have realized that you have made your sacrifices in your own ways. I have simply been unable to see it. I now return your friendship back to you."

Soon enough, the god of sleep disappeared.

The samurai and dragon looked at each other. They suddenly felt a source of strength that they had never felt before.

"Are you ready for another battle?" the dragon asked haughtily.

"You bet," the samurai replied.

They leaped against each other, twisting and turning to outsmart the other. Just like they had dreamed, the samurai had gotten faster, and the dragon had gotten swifter.

"Just like I imagined," the samurai said.

"Same to you, my friend," the dragon replied.

Soon enough, the animals in the forest had gathered to look at the beautiful sight.

Like so many days and nights before, the samurai and dragon heaved as they realized they had expended all their energy.

"You've been sharpening your sword, my friend," the dragon said.

"Well, your scales have been getting harder," said the samurai.

"You ready for a nap?" asked the dragon.

"Another match right after?" asked the samurai.

"You bet," the dragon replied.

They lay against each other staring at the night sky, which was glistening with stars and the full moon.

As they fell asleep, they returned their richest dreams to the god of sleep.

**

During my freshmen year at Harvard, I decided to take a chemistry course since I had enjoyed the discipline in high school. This was a terrible mistake.

While I already had four extracurriculars and a full course load, I was unwilling to sacrifice my social life with friends and my personal hobbies like playing piano and painting. I was already barely finishing the weekly problem sets for class, let alone the preparing for the upcoming midterms and weekly labs. It was here that I began cutting into my designated sleeping time to have more time to study.

On the day of the final exam, I remember leaving the exam room and going straight to the closest bathroom stall, ready to wail my eyes out. I knew that I had failed it. While I had answered each question as well as I could, I noticed the holes in my studies. While the content was difficult, I knew I could've performed better on the final exam had I allowed myself more time to study the material throughout the semester.

When I decided to study Chinese during my sophomore year at college, I was reminded of the importance of sleep. Unlike many of the other courses that had a couple of midterms and final exams throughout the semester, Chinese had dictations a couple times a week. I was tested on my rote memorization skills to write Chinese characters, understand their meanings, and speak the words with correct intonations a couple of times a week.

As the semester progressed, I came to realize that sleeping was vital for my success in the classroom. How often I studied the words and how much sleep I got beforehand could drastically impact my quiz results. One day, I remember having studied for the vocab quiz for about five hours before heading directly into the classroom. I thought I was ready. As the Chinese *laoshi*, or teacher, read out the words, I remember my hands shaking uncontrollably as I realized that I could not recollect any of the words that I had studied all night.

Through it all, I learned that I needed to strategize my sleep in the same way I had planned out my class schedule, club meetings, and lunch dates with friends. Sleep was no longer a habit but a strategy for academic success.

Small habits add up. Over time, I realized that my dictation scores were heavily dependent on the amount and quality of sleep I had gotten in addition to the actual number of hours

I spent studying.

In light of this reality, this chapter attempts to convince our society that we must guide citizens to strategize sleep, not sacrifice it, in order to succeed. While we have seen how emerging markets have been trying to offer innovative products to control sleep in Chapter 4 and how companies have been offering various services to promote better-quality sleep in Chapter 5, this chapter discusses how sleep trends and cultures may change at a more fundamental level.

Sleep Cities

In 2015, Joan Faus Vitoria — mayor of the town Ador within the province of Valencia, Spain — issued an edict that town residents be able to take a nap between 2 p.m. and 5 p.m. This meant that parents had to keep their children indoors during those hours while residents and tourists were instructed to avoid making unnecessary noise. With only 1,400 inhabitants in Ador, the main purpose of the edict was to ensure that the agricultural workers would not toil in the heat during the hottest hours of the day. With a temperature of about 104 degrees Fahrenheit, people are "recommended to spend their times indoors to avoid the heat waves."

Spain is not the only country with the concept of *siestas*, although it is uncommon for a town to actually issue an edict regarding sleep. Countries like the Philippines, China, India, Greece, Bangladesh, and Italy have midday rests. Many places in Latin America close businesses between 2 p.m. and 4 p.m. to accommodate siestas.

Some cities, however, have been taking the sleep experiment to a new level.

In a German spa town called Bad Kissingen, Dr. Thomas Kantermann has started the ChronoCity Project, which attempts to "promote the town's health through sleep." Kantermann pays attention to "urban lighting scheme, changing school and work times and improving the overall conditions for shift workers and hospital patients."

A large portion of the project is inspired by chronobiology, a science that studies how our internal clocks interact with time cues in the environment. Not surprisingly — as also suggested by Chapter 3 — every human "chronotype" is different, meaning that while individuals have certain hours of the day that they are most productive and active, they differ among people.

The concept of chronobiology stems from a 1729 experiment by astronomer Jean-Jacques d'Ortous de Mairan, who found that the leaves of his heliotrope plant closed and opened at the same time each day regardless of whether the sun was present or not. Curious as to whether this pattern would be replicated in humans, German biologist Jürgen Aschoff observed that humans placed inside an underground bunker without access to light, sound, or Earth's vibrations would keep to a 24-hour schedule.

If Bad Kissingen succeeds in its plans, it will become the first city to utilize chronobiology and other sleep science to enhance the well-being and productivity of a population. While the town has only 20,000 inhabitants, there is also the potential to influence the 250,000 tourists who visit the area annually. Currently, European spa towns are competing to figure out their competitive edge in the tourism industry. Bad Kissingen's competitive edge comes in the form of its 17 health hospitals, sanatoriums, and rehab centers, making it the perfect place to start a "sleep city." There is no doubt that there will be a plethora of obstacles along the way, as the city will still need to track the sleep data of all the residents in Bad Kissingen to see if its plan is effective or not.

POLYPHASIC SLEEP

Perhaps the problem is that our bodies were never designed to sleep eight hours and wake for 16 in the first place. Pet owners know well that their beloved dog or cat is quite often snuggled up for a nap at any hour of the day or night. They also know that their pets sleep late and wake up early, rarely sleeping soundly for the full length of time we humans might sleep. This observation fits in with other observations from throughout the animal kingdom: Most animals practice polyphasic sleep, with multiple small intervals of sleep interspersed between periods of wakefulness.

Babies tend to practice polyphasic sleep to some degree, sleeping multiple times during the day and waking up throughout the night (to the chagrin of mothers). Even humans in times past have had similar patterns of sleep. Roger Ekirch has established a career looking at the history of sleep habits, and his book *At Day's Close: Night in Times Past* documents how humans in the past slept twice during the night.

Knowing this, researchers have done experiments in which human research subjects lived in constricted environments devoid of time cues, using artificial light or none at all, eliminating references to time or activity, and allowing them to eat and sleep whenever they choose. One study found that people in this environment tend to sleep in 3.5-hour nap intervals evenly distributed throughout the day, while staying awake five hours at a time.

Variations on this idea of sleeping many times a day have arisen over the years. Initially referred to as the Uberman Sleep Schedule, one polyphasic sleep strategy introduced in a blog called "everything2" suggested that people could train themselves to sleep only three hours a day by distributing six 30-minute sleeping sessions equally throughout the day. Although the blog posted that the schedule is a "potentially dangerous way to increase your waking hours," the concept gained enormous popularity.

The reality, however, is that no matter how appealing polyphasic sleep sounds, research suggests that humans cannot adapt to just any sleeping pattern. There are only two ideal options: 1) the full 6-8 hours per night or 2) 5-7 hours per night with a 15-90 minute nap.

But for all the reasons discussed in previous chapters, sleeping in this way is not feasible for many. Whether it's due to the fact you enjoy the flexibility of choosing your own hours or the fact that unpopular working shifts offer higher pay, workers are finding that they are no longer tied to the typical 9-to-5 work day. Perhaps a sleep revolution is needed, and some people may benefit from a variation of polyphasic sleep in times of dire need.

HARVARD TIME

As the oldest institution in the United States, Harvard College has nearly 400 years worth of traditions, and many Harvard students have debated how valuable or meaningful these different traditions truly are. One tradition that I thought was counterintuitive but necessary for my own survival was "Harvard Time," which allows students to arrive seven minutes late to classes, extracurricular activities, or just about any meeting at the College. As much as the concept of Harvard Time is interesting in itself, there is an equally interesting story behind Harvard's seven-minute delays.

The story of Harvard Time starts with women who attended Radcliffe College, the female coordinate school for Harvard College. While women studied at Harvard as early as 1879 through the "Harvard Annex," they did not have access to an official campus with dorms until the 1920s. As the women's campus was about a half mile away, it took women about seven minutes to walk from class in Radcliffe to Harvard Yard. To prevent students from being late to class, Harvard Time was born, and soon all students took advantage of this built-in delay to make it to class.

Many years later, I lay in bed looking at the clock, calculating how many more minutes I could squeeze out before heading out to class. Constantly sleep-deprived, I heavily relied on Harvard Time to make ends meet. After suffering through chemistry and Chinese class, I saw firsthand how Harvard Time was actually making me do worse. In a way, Harvard seemed to reverse all the habits I had spent years perfecting. As a sophomore in high school, I still remember nervously looking at my watch as I prepared for an interview for my first internship. With the fickle Los Angeles public transportation system, I could not trust the bus to get me to the unfamiliar buildings in Century City on time. I made such an effort to be punctual that I ended up being an hour early to my interview.

Perhaps after seeing its students' performance decline, Harvard has expressed interest in phasing out Harvard Time. Last year, Harvard's campus newspaper, *The Crimson*, reported that the university intends to increase the time between classes to remove the seven-minute grace time that students use to excuse their tardiness. According to the Dean of Undergraduate Studies, Jay Harris, students have reported that Harvard Time "detracts from the sense of seriousness" in academics.

Not surprisingly, my friends expressed similar critiques during my time on campus. Sarcastic comments like "Employers are going to love us Harvard students, always coming seven minutes late to meetings" or "The university sure does a great job of preparing us for the real world" were common among my peers, and we joked about the absurdity of it all.

At the end of the day, they are right! Harvard is finally catching up. The administration has realized that students have to be prepared for a world where there is no Harvard Time, a world that already exists outside the bubble of Harvard Yard.

Similarly, we have been lulled into the perception that we can cheat on sleep. As we have seen, this is clearly not the solution to the increasing demands of society. We need to learn how to take care of ourselves so that we can be the best versions of ourselves. We need to think of how to cheat on wakefulness instead, with power naps and sleep technology.

It will take time for society to change and better accommodate healthy sleeping habits and for siestas and sleep cities to be available to every worker. In the meantime, take a nap.

Chapter Summary:

- Surprise, America! Societies can actually encourage sleep so that people can be more productive!
- Sleep trends can be harmful for people, but they can also be effective if used properly.
- Make it a habit to get more sleep. Strategize your naps. They will help you.

PART 3

CONCLUSION

If you don't sleep, you cannot achieve your dream. I mean this in both a figurative and literal sense.

When I was growing up, my mother would often retell the story of how I got my Korean name, *Sooho Lee*. Before my mother knew that she was pregnant, she had a dream where she found three tigers lurking inside the forest. She still remembers how she wasn't scared at the sight of the three tigers. The tiger on the right was the most handsome creature she had seen and she thought to herself, "I wish I could have that tiger as my own." In the blink of an eye, that tiger was the only tiger in front of her.

Before she could think about the oddity of the event, she woke up.

Later on, she realized that she had a *taemong*, a precognitive dream about the birth of a child. Perhaps because it is commonly expected in Korea for parents to have precognitive dreams of their children, many South Koreans have stories of *taemong*. Soon after my mother realized that she had me in her womb, my father had another dream. He was busily walking through the mountainous forest with a boar he had caught when he ran into a tiger. He remembers offering the boar to the tiger. Quickly, the tiger ate the boar before going into a deep slumber. From his dream, my father remembers being content looking at the sleeping tiger.

When I was born, my mother decided to give me an English name because I was her first child to be born in America. However, to remember my Korean roots, she put my Korean name as my middle name. My Korean name means "remarkable tiger."

Thinking back on this story, I realize that her sleep created my name, my identity that would remain with me for the rest of my life.

My mother's story often fascinated me as a child because I could not believe that she had dreamt my birth before she knew that she was pregnant. The concept of a precognitive dream itself is fascinating because of its exoticism and fantasy-like elements. To this day, I am skeptical of the gigantic dream book with over a thousand pages on our bookshelf listing thousands of dreams that decipher our future. And yet, it's fun. I still remember the days my sister and I would rush over to the book if either of us had had an interesting dream the previous night.

It urged my sister and me to open and actively read the book that took many generations of our superstitious ancestors and a diligent writer to produce.

This book is about sleep and productivity. However, I have a deeper message that I would like to relay: Without fun and without passion, we cannot reach our maximum potentials.

And that fun and passion comes from sleep. By napping, daydreaming, and counting sheep, you can make your dreams a reality. Sleep changes your personality, your emotions, and your brain activity. It helps consolidate the information you have collected throughout the day and structure your thoughts in a way that is meaningful and valuable to you. It helps you be better in your sport, your instrument, and your creative projects.

Yes, there may be nights where you need to and want to sacrifice your sleep for your term paper, your passion project, or your job. There may be times in your life where you have no choice but to get a part-time job as an Uber driver and sacrifice your sleep to make ends meet.

However, at the end of the day, without ample sleep, your are literally forgoing your dreams.

I admit that our world doesn't make sleeping easy. From bustling city life to the cutthroat culture of school and the workplace, it is easy to make sleep your last priority. At times, some people don't have access to dark and cool rooms or the hours in the day to squeeze in nap time, let alone a full eight-hour sleep. These are some of our social problems with no easy solutions.

However, hopefully through this book, you have found solutions that may help with your sleep journey. Today, our apps bring us food, do our laundry, provide valet services for our cars, and ship our clothes as well as offer us ways to return them. In a world where presentation matters as much as content, CEOs have personal coaches for vocal practices and personal shoppers to fill up every second of their nap. With products like Blue Apron on the market, even the occasional cooking experience is simplified by offering precisely measured groceries for the perfectly picturesque meal from start to finish.

Similarly, our world today has nap pods, sleep apps, sleep cities, and napping cafes, just to name a few sleep innovations.

We also have a wide array of rolling alarm clocks, Ostrich Pillows, and Suitsies.

It's time to start a more active dialogue around sleep so that we can take advantage of such innovations. As I mentioned in my introduction, we need to allow for a cultural exchange using a common dialogue to discuss a growing worldwide phenomenon: sleep loss. Let's create a world where we have more time for ourselves to grow physically, emotionally, and psychologically. Let's create a world of slumber, even if just for 20 additional minutes. If there's anything I hope you take away from this book, it's that our world needs more sleep.

It is my firm belief that small changes can have drastic results. During the construction of the Golden Gate Bridge, there were both Irish and Chinese immigrants laboring for the construction project. However, employers noticed that the Irish immigrants would get sick more often. Why? Were the Chinese biologically healthier? Was it in their genes?

No. We later found that the Irish workers were dying from the polluted water on the work site.

Well, how did the Chinese workers solve the problem?

They boiled water.

Today, we know that Chinese workers were more fit for this particular environment because they were able to kill harmful bacteria in the the polluted waters at the working site.

However — in the same way that the Chinese workers boiled dirty water — nap pods, our sleep aids, and other innovations are helping us make some of our ends meet. With an understanding of the current sleep industries in Asia and the few pockets of U.S. cities, employers and individuals can imagine a different world where they have a better relationship with sleep. People assume that professionalism is a result of their hard work. And to a certain extent, they are right: You cannot achieve greatness without hard work. However, small habits also have profound effects on one's performance. Recognizing this fact is the first step in improving your or your team's productivity levels.

The small habit we want you to add is sleep. We want you to dream, to nap. To me, there is no doubt that my parents' dreams and various dreams that I had as a child have had profound impacts on who I am today.

Every day, what you encounter, what you experience, what you eat and drink, and what you do have a profound impact on who you become. Likewise, you choose how you sleep, defining the perfect sleep experience to meet your needs. These are the experiences that you choose to define you every day.

Remember, sleep is the source of our potential strength and untapped essence.

Use your sleep as a weapon! It is the samurai's sword. Use sleep to rise up to the pinnacle of your career. You are the slumbering dragon waiting to rise up to the sky.

How will you sleep today?

ACKNOWLEDGEMENTS

I have received so much love, support, and guidance to complete this book. This book would not have been possible without the help of my sister, Claryce, and her husband, Yu-Ming. Many thanks to Julia DeAngelo for lending an extra pair of eyes to copyedit my book. Many thanks to Terry Cralle, certified clinical sleep educator and author of *Sleeping Your Way to the Top*, for being my first interviewee for my book and inspiring me to continue my project. Incredible thanks to Eric Koester, Brian Bies, Anastasia Armendariz, and the New Degree Publishing staff, who all helped me make this book a reality. Thank you to the many others who have helped me throughout my journey. Without all your help, I would not be person I am today.

SELECTED BIBLIOGRAPHY

Introduction:

Peela, Ravi Teja Venkata. "What are the best day-to-day time-saving tips?" *Quora*. March 9, 2014. <https://www.quora.com/What-are-the-best-day-to-day-time-saving-tips/answer/Ravi-Teja-Venkata-Peela>. Web. 7 July 2017.

Chapter 1:

Popova, Maria. "Thomas Edison, Power-Napper: The Great Inventor on Sleep and Success." *Brain Pickings*. Amazon Services LLC Associates Program, 11 Feb. 2016. Web.

Cushman, Chloe. "Book Excerpt: How the Lightbulb Transformed the Way We Sleep."*National Post*. Special to National Post, 17 Sept. 2012. Web.

Jenkins, Logan. "Mozart of Sleep Helped Adults Wake up to Student Biology." *The San Diego Union-Tribune*. The San Diego Union-Tribune, 15 Mar. 2017. Web.

Reiss, Benjamin. "Sleeping Through the Night Is a Relatively New Invention." *Science of Us*. Vintage Images/Getty Images, 8 Mar. 2017. Web.

Kapitalust. "The Fallacy of Romanticizing the Past." Blog post. *Kapitalust*. Kapitalust, 28 Oct. 2016. Web.

Chapter 2:

"Three Steps Ahead: The South Korean Beauty Market." *Mintel*. Mintel, 23 Oct. 2014. Web.

Wright, Pam. "South Korea's Obsession With Plastic Surgery Leads To A $5 Billion Industry."*The Inquisitr*. The Inquisitr, 12 Sept. 2015. Web. 10 July 2017.

Thayer, R. (1996) "The origin of Everyday Moods." Oxford, Oxford University Press.

Steger, Isabella. "After 20 Years of Studying and Exams, South Korea's Smartest Graduates Struggle to Find a Job." *Quartz*. Quartz, 16 Oct. 2016. Web.

Lee, Claire. "Youth Unemployment Rate in Korea Reaches Highest in 15 Years." *The Korea Herald*. The Korea Herald, 26 July 2015. Web.

Biddle, Jeff E., and Daniel S. Hamermesh. "Wage Discrimination over the Business Cycle." *IZA Journal of Labor Policy*. Springer Berlin Heidelberg, 01 July 2013.

Cralle, Terry, William David Brown, and William Cane. *Sleeping Your Way to the Top: How to Get the Sleep You Need to Succeed*. New York, NY: Sterling, 2016. Print.

Brassfield, Marissa. "Beauty and Salary: How Does Employee Attractiveness Affect Lifetime Pay." *Career News*. PayScale Human Capital, 23 June 2016. Web.

Clark, Stephanie. "Does Sleep Make You More Attractive?" *Sleep Outfitters*. Sleep Outfitters, 23 July 2015. Web.

"Sleep Really Does Make You Prettier." *Cosmopolitan*. Cosmopolitan, 16 Nov. 2016. Web.

Phillips, Bradley G., Masahiko Kato, Krzysztof Narkiewicz, Ian Choe, and Virend K. Somers. "Increases in Leptin Levels, Sympathetic

Drive, and Weight Gain in Obstructive Sleep Apnea." *American Journal of Physiology - Heart and Circulatory Physiology*. American Physiological Society, 01 July 2000. Web.

Adams, Gerard. "What Is Emotional Intelligence and Why Does It Matter?" *Entrepreneur*. Entrepreneur, 13 May 2016. Web.

Perry, Susan. "A Poor Night's Sleep May Raise Risk of Catching a Cold, Study Suggests." *MinnPost*. MinnPost, 3 Sept. 2015. Web.

"Government Group Looks To Prevent Drowsy Driving Crashes." *CBS New York*. CBS New York, 20 Mar. 2017. Web.

Nowak, Claire. "Sleep Apnea: Why Snoring Is a Dangerous Symptom." *Reader's Digest*. Reader's Digest, 07 Mar. 2017. Web.

Smith, Chris. "Uber Suspends Self-driving Car Program after Bizarre Accident." *BGR*. BGR, 27 Mar. 2017. Web.

[CBS This Morning]. (2015, September 28). *Behind the plastic surgery boom in South Korea* [Video File]. Retrieved from https://www.youtube.com/watch?v=ZSA0ETxubSI

"How Long Can Humans Stay Awake?" *Scientific American*. Scientific American, 25 Mar. 2002. Web.

Chapter 3:

Stulberg, Brad, and Steve Magness. *Peak Performance: Elevate Your Game, Avoid Burnout, and Thrive with the New Science of Success.* Emmaus, PA: Rodale, 2017. Print.

Griffiths, Sarah. "Early Risers and Night Owls Have Structural Brain Differences: Discovery Could Help Explain Why People Late to Bed Can Suffer from a Form of 'chronic Jet Lag.'" *Daily Mail Online.* Associated Newspapers, 02 Oct. 2013. Web.

Deshpande, Madhavi. "Why Can't Parents Make Teenagers Sleep Early At Night?" *Science ABC.* Science ABC, 12 Jan. 2017. Web.

Kanazawa, Satoshi. "Why Night Owls Are More Intelligent Than Morning Larks." *Psychology Today.* Sussex Publishers, 09 May 2010. Web.

Martin, Lauren. "Intelligent People All Have One Thing In Common: They Stay Up Later Than You." *Elite Daily.* Elite Daily, 13 Aug. 2015. Web.

"What Is Good Quality Sleep?" *EurekaAlert.* The Global Source for Science News, 23 Jan. 2017. Web.

Swayne, Matthew. "Masculinity, Sleep Deprivation Lead to Health,

Safety Issues." *Penn State University*. Penn State University, 9 Jan. 2014. Web.

Kuang, Cliff. "Infographic Of The Day: Why Pro Athletes Sleep 12 Hours A Day." *Co.Design*. Co.Design, 28 Apr. 2017. Web.

Plunkett, Mike. "A Machine That Used to Be Considered Punishment Is Now a $1.4 Billion Fitness Industry." *The Washington Post*. WP Company, 31 Jan. 2017. Web.

"Donald Trump's Four Hours a Night and the Other Extreme Sleeping Habits of Our Leaders." *The Telegraph*. Telegraph Media Group, 09 Feb. 2017. Web.

"Jeff Bezos: Why Getting 8 Hours of Sleep Is Good for Amazon Shareholders." *Thrive Global*. Thrive Global, 30 Nov. 2016. Web. 10 July 2017.

Roth, Carol. "Sleep In and Make Millions: Why You Don't Need to Wake Up at 5 A.M." *Entrepreneur*. Entrepreneur, 17 Apr. 2017. Web.

Chapter 4:

Dvorsky, George. "The Science behind Power Naps, and Why They're so Damn Good for You." *Io9*. Io9.gizmodo.com, 26 Sept. 2013. Web.

"Using a Neck Pillow to Reduce Neck Pain." *EverydayHealth.com*. Everyday Health, 07 May 2009. Web.

Owen, Jonathan. "Thai Billionaire Who Invented Red Bull Energy Drink Dies in Bangkok, Aged 89." *The Independent*. Independent Digital News and Media, 17 Mar. 2012. Web.

Owen, Jonathan. "Thai Billionaire Who Invented Red Bull Energy Drink Dies in Bangkok, Aged 89." *The Independent*. Independent Digital News and Media, 17 Mar. 2012. Web.

"Drink Neuro: Functional Beverage Review." *Caffeine Informer*. Caffeine Informer, n.d. Web. 10 July 2017.

Syam, Piyali. "The Dark Side and Downsides of Melatonin." *Van Winkle's*. Van Winkle's, 17 Dec. 2015. Web.

Ferenstein, Greg. "A Hands-On Review of Suitsy, the Silicon Valley Onesie Suit." *Gizmodo*. Gizmodo.com, 17 May 2015. Web. 10 July 2017.

Silverman, Justin R. "Goodbye Three-piece Suit, Hello One-piece Suit: Meet Suitsy, the Business Suit Onesie." *TODAY.com*. TODAY, 25 Jan. 2016. Web.

Chapter 5:

Green, Penelope. "Sleep Is the New Status Symbol." *The New York Times*. The New York Times, 08 Apr. 2017. Web.

Kuang, Cliff. "Infographic Of The Day: Why Pro Athletes Sleep 12 Hours A Day." *Co.Design*. Co.Design, 28 Apr. 2017. Web.

Jakovljević, Branko, Goran Belojević, Katarina Paunović, and Vesna Stojanov. "Road Traffic Noise and Sleep Disturbances in an Urban Population: Cross-sectional Study." *Croatian Medical Journal*. Croatian Medical Schools, Feb. 2006. Web. 10

"Sleep in the City." *Sleep Education*. American Academy of Sleep Medicine, 26 Sept. 2008. Web.

"World's Population Increasingly Urban with More than Half Living in Urban Areas | UN DESA Department of Economic and Social Affairs." *United Nations*. United Nations, 10 July 2014. Web.

Giaimo, Cara. "The Doomed Mouse Utopia That Inspired the 'Rats of NIMH.'" *Atlas Obscura*. Atlas Obscura, 30 Sept. 2016. Web.

Garnett, Carla. "Medical Historian Examines NIMH Experiments in Crowding - The NIH Record -July 25, 2008." *National Institutes of Health*. U.S. Department of Health and Human Services, 25 July 2008. Web.

Filloon, Whitney. "Tokyo's New Nap Cafe Is an Actual Dream Come True." *Eater*. Eater, 20 Mar. 2017. Web.

"Coffee Naps: The Bulletproof Power Nap, Explained." *Bulletproof*. Bulletproof, 13 Apr. 2017. Web.

Doheny, Kathleen. "Sleep Less, Eat More?" *WebMD*. WebMD, 14 Mar. 2012. Web.

Chapter 6:

Hall, John. "Mayor Says Children Must Be Kept inside between 2pm and 5pm and Tells Town to Be Quiet as It Becomes the First in Spain to Have an Official Afternoon Nap Time." *Daily Mail Online*. Associated Newspapers, 17 July 2015. Web.

"The ChronoCity Project: Using Chronobiology to Change Behavior." *Chronobiology*. Chronobiology, 24 Jan. 2017. Web.

Beck, Julie. "The Town That's Building Life Around Sleep." *The Atlantic*. Atlantic Media Company, 05 Feb. 2014. Web.

Uno, Jessica. "The German Town That's Revolutionizing Sleep." *Sleep Junkies*. Sleep Junkies, 14 Apr. 2014. Web.

Campbell, S. S. and Tobler, I. Animal sleep: a review of sleep duration across phylogeny. *Neurosci. Biobehav. Rev.*, 1984, 8: 269–300. W.W. Norton, 2005

Campbell SS, Murphy PJ. The nature of spontaneous sleep across adulthood. J Sleep Res. 2007 Mar;16(1):24-32. PubMed PMID: 17309760.

PureDoxyk. "Uberman's Sleep Schedule." *Everything2.* Everything2.com, 29 Dec. 2000. Web.

Wozniak, Piotr. "Polyphasic Sleep: Facts and Myths." *SuperMemo.* SuperMemo, Jan. 2005. Web. 10 July 2017.

Rodman, Melissa C. "Allston Move Could Mean the End of 'Harvard Time.'" *The Harvard Crimson.* The Harvard Crimson, 5 Apr. 2016. Web.

Vanni, Olivia. "'Harvard Time' Is On the Chopping Block." *BostInno.* BostInno, 05 Apr. 2016. Web.

Book Cover:

Cover dragon illustration by Angelus on Wikimedia Commons.

Cover samurai illustration by Teruhisa Osawa and Kuniyoshi Kubota on Japanvector.

Cover author photo by Arthur Nguyen.

Made in the USA
Middletown, DE
24 October 2017